D1178024

meditation
the cool way to calm

meditation
the cool way to calm

john selby

TUTTLE PUBLISHING
Boston · Rutland, Vermont · Tokyo

First published in 2004 by Tuttle Publishing, an imprint of Periplus Editions
(HK) Ltd., with editorial offices at 153 Milk Street, Boston, Massachusetts
02109.

Copyright © 2004 John Selby

ISBN 0-8048-3486-5
Library of Congress Control Number: 2003115384

Distributed by

North America, Latin America
& Europe
Tuttle Publishing
Distribution Center
Airport Industrial Park
364 Innovation Drive
North Clarendon, VT 05759-9436
Tel: (802) 773-8930
Fax: (802) 773-6993
info@tuttlepublishing.com
www.tuttlepublishing.com

Asia Pacific
Berkeley Books Pte. Ltd.
130 Joo Seng Road
#06-01/03 Olivine Building
Singapore 368357
Tel: (65) 6280-1330
Fax: (65) 6280-6290
inquiries@periplus.com.sg

Japan
Tuttle Publishing
Yaekari Building, 3rd Floor
5-4-12 Osaki
Shinagawa-ku
Tokyo 141 0032
Tel: (03) 5437-0171
Fax: (03) 5437-0755
tuttle-sales@gol.com

First edition
08 07 06 05 04   10 9 8 7 6 5 4 3 2 1
Design by Linda Carey
Printed in the Canada

CONTENTS

Author's Note		*7*
Prologue		*10*

Part One
Breath Awareness (Starting on the Path)   **19**

Chapter 1	What Is Meditation?	20
Chapter 2	Where Did Meditation Come From?	26
Chapter 3	Learning to Find Your Breath	32
Chapter 4	What Will Your Parents Think?	37
Chapter 5	How Does Meditation Work?	42
Chapter 6	Expanding Your Consciousness	49
Meditation One	*The Breath Meditation*	*54*

Part Two
Heart Awareness (Dealing with Emotions)   **57**

Chapter 7	Opening to Feelings	58
Chapter 8	Healing Heartbreaks	63
Chapter 9	Moving Through Emotions	66
Chapter 10	Understanding Your Feelings	76
Chapter 11	Dealing With Your Parents	85
Chapter 12	And Suddenly . . . Peace of Mind	93
Meditation Two	*Heart Awakening*	*99*

Part Three
Mind Awareness (Learning the 7 Focus Phrases)   **101**

Chapter 13	Thoughts and Emotions	103
Chapter 14	How Our Minds Really Work	108

Chapter 15   Heart and Mind Together   116
Chapter 16   Meditative Focus Phrases   122
Chapter 17   Quieting Your Mind   128
Chapter 18   Loving Yourself—Really   132
Chapter 19   Opening to Heal   139

Meditation Three   *Quiet Mind/Open Heart*   *145*

Part Four
Self-Awareness (Overcoming Obstacles)   **149**

Chapter 20   Ending Emotional Suffering   151
Chapter 21   Having Faith in Your Practice   157
Chapter 22   Letting Go of Judgment   164
Chapter 23   Walking the Path Together   170

Meditation Four   *Insight and Discovery*   *179*

Part Five
Special Cool-Calm Meditations   **181**

Quick Meditation Uplift (1 minute)   182
The Basic Cool-Calm Meditation (10 minutes)   183
Intuition: Resolving Life's Problems   184
Emotions: Calming Anger and Worries   188
Relating: Healing Heartbreaks   192
Love: Opening to Deep Sharing   197
Wisdom: Discovering Who You Really Are   203

Final Words: Meditation in Action   *208*

Sharing What You Learn   *211*

References and Further Reading   *219*

AUTHOR'S NOTE

There is nothing more intimate and important to us than our inner thoughts and emotions. And there is nothing quite so upsetting as being tormented by our thoughts and suffering from out-of-control feelings. Especially during our teen years, it sometimes seems we're on a crazy emotional roller-coaster ride that just won't stop—all sorts of bothersome and upsetting thoughts keep racing through our minds, which in turn stimulate feelings of confusion, anger, worry, shame, and guilt. Is there nothing we can do to gain control of our minds, to break free from the emotions that upset us, and to begin to live our lives with more confidence, clarity, peace, and fun?

I was lucky enough to grow up in a town in California where a most wonderful meditation teacher, Krishnamurti, spent half of each year. By the time I entered high school I had learned how to meditate and had a beginning notion of how to take charge of my own mind. This powerful tool of meditation helped me through my teen years. I would like to show you, as you now come of age and claim your place in the adult world, how, in a totally nonreligious way, you can learn to manage your thoughts and feelings to your advantage. I would like to share with you, as I have with my own teenagers, a very simple yet wonderfully effective new approach to mastering the fine art of meditation.

The term meditation means different things to different people. For me, meditation isn't about religious beliefs or spiritual rituals. It's about specific things you can do with your mind to make your life flow better. When we put away all the esoteric religious trappings usually associated with meditating, and get down to meditation's logical psychological foundation, we find that meditation is clearly the most powerful and enjoyable mental tool ever invented.

The easy-to-learn approach to meditation I'll be teaching in this book will enable you to take charge of your mind and break free from your emotional aches and mental confusions. As you learn to aim your almighty power of attention, your life will brighten up and take off in directions that you yourself consciously choose.

Put away that stereotype of a bearded guru meditating in some far-off cave in the Himalayan wilderness. Meditation is something you can do anywhere, anytime—while taking a walk, in school before an exam, while playing sports, while out on a date—whenever you want to calm down, get clear, and enjoy life more. This meditation technique works in any situation and during any time frame—not only as a daily half-hour practice but also as a ten-minute reflection break, a four-minute breather, and, yes, even a one-minute CoolCalm quickie when you need to instantly calm down, get centered, clear your mind . . . and then leap back into action.

This new short-form approach to meditation might make some traditional meditators shake their heads, but as you'll find out for yourself, it works absolutely perfectly, allowing you to take meditation anywhere you need its quick powerful boost of emotional calm and mental clarity. You will now have in hand a practical way to help yourself succeed in life.

Right from the very first pages of this book, you'll discover that this isn't by any means a traditional instruction book on meditation. Instead, to show you how the power and practice of meditation can become a practical part of your everyday life, this book will move back and forth between an engrossing story of high schoolers applying meditation to their lives, and short reflective discussions that will help you understand meditation. Why are we using this format for exploring meditation? First of all, it's just more fun to learn through reading about real-life situations. And second, the dramatic format is simply more effective— you'll find that right in the middle of an enjoyable story about high schoolers like yourself, you're also learning how to meditate.

Here's another thing about the kind of meditation you'll learn in this book: Nobody needs to even know that you're doing it. All they'll see is that right in the middle of being upset or confused or otherwise emotionally and mentally a mess, you're suddenly able to regain your composure, let go of your feelings, and attain a sense of personal balance and power. You are now able to perform at your optimum, relate with strength and compassion, and in general succeed in whatever you're doing at the moment.

As you'll see with the life stories in the following chapters, learning to meditate can change your life for the better—and it's not that hard to master. Within a few weeks you'll be able to do these meditations successfully and discover your inner power to transform your life in ways that you yourself choose.

You'll notice that throughout this book we often talk about how your parents might respond to your reading and learning about meditation and how to actually do it. You might want to consider letting your parents read this book, too—they'll especially like the parts where the parents in the story become actively involved in the drama—and they can of course also learn how to meditate from this book. It works for everyone.

So, enough introduction. Without further ado, let's get right into the story.

PROLOGUE

Julie felt nervous as she headed to the party. Danny would probably be there, and considering the abrupt way he'd said "Hi" to her and then gone off with his friends in school today, she didn't know what to expect of him at all. Was he being moody, or did he just not want to be friends with her anymore?

As she walked up the front steps of the house she could hear loud music. Her stomach felt queasy and she wished she hadn't dressed so sexy. She wanted to be attractive for Danny, but maybe he'd get the wrong idea. She thought of just turning around and heading back home; she was under pressure from her dad to raise her grades and she needed to study biology all weekend. But the idea of going home wasn't all that appealing either—her parents were having one of their big arguments and she preferred to be out of the house when that happened. Besides, she was afraid that if she didn't go to the party, Danny might flirt with other girls—so she walked inside with uncertainty.

Danny was standing with some of his buddies talking about a movie when Julie came through the front door. He immediately tensed—she looked so good! What did she expect? What would he do? So far he'd hardly had the nerve to even kiss her goodnight. Part of him wanted to head right over to her as she stood a moment chatting with some of her friends. But he felt frozen, afraid to go move—and before he could push through his hesitancies, she was walking right on through the room, not even noticing him, and out the sliding-glass door that lead to the backyard.

Julie gave a sigh of relief as she stepped out of the house and away from the loud music and the room crammed with partygoers. She much preferred the relative peace and quiet of the backyard.

As she was chatting with a couple friends, a relatively new girl at school came by and joined them. She was introduced as Lisa. The high school was so big, there were loads of people Julie didn't know, but this girl instantly sparked Julie's attention; she had an unusual peaceful quality to her expression, and she wasn't pushy at all.

Ten minutes later, the two of them were under a big tree drinking Cokes and talking. Julie envied Lisa's effortless calm, and the subtle but really knockout beautiful way she smiled. A couple of boys came by and goofed off with them, interested in Lisa as much as Julie, or even more. And then suddenly there was Danny. Julie's breathing got tense; she felt dizzy as she walked off with him to dance.

"I'll see you sometime, okay?" she said to Lisa, smiling and hoping she wasn't hurting her feelings by suddenly leaving her.

Lisa nodded with a return smile. Julie hoped she'd found a new friend, but she hardly had time to think about Lisa the rest of the evening. She and Danny danced together, or rather banged around the floor of the big living room, and glanced into each other's eyes now and then. Then a boy in Julie's history class wanted to dance with her, and when she finally said yes to him, Danny just disappeared.

As soon as the song was over, Julie went looking for Danny. Her heart was pounding, she was afraid of what she might find, of being rejected, and sure enough when she found Danny, he was in the kitchen chatting with a girl, just the two of them alone, sipping drinks and munching on chips. Julie turned around and quickly walked out, hoping Danny hadn't seen her, but he had.

Julie went into the bathroom and locked herself in, feeling ready to cry. Finally, when someone knocked on the door, she managed to pull her emotions together enough to unlock the door, ready to walk quickly out of the party and go home, but there was Danny standing there, waiting for her.

"So how was your new romance?" she asked him.

"Well, how was yours?" he said right back.

They stared each other down. She felt on the verge of crying again, her breathing caught in her throat and her temperature boiling.

"Anyway," he said, "I'm heading home."

"Me too."

And so they left the party together and walked down the street. It was fairly late, and everything was quiet once they got around the corner from the party. They didn't say anything for a while. Then he came to a stop.

"So, you know that guy?" he said, his voice tense, almost accusing.

"Oh, just in class."

"Hmm."

"Hmm what?" she insisted.

"Hey, you can dance with whoever you want, we're not going together or anything."

"Danny, I don't like it when you get mad at me. I didn't do anything."

He stood there, not saying a word.

"I like you, you know that, better than anyone else," she said quietly, her heart pounding in her chest as she risked being honest.

"Well, that's mutual," he said gruffly.

She smiled at him, then came gently against him, not thinking, just spontaneously. For a moment they were softly together, arms around each other. Then she felt him squeezing her against him, and his lips came down against hers. She was caught so off guard that she pushed back.

"Hey, sorry," he muttered, and before she could catch her breath to say anything, he turned around and hurried away through the night.

Monday morning Julie came out of her biology exam a wreck, afraid she'd done terribly. And Danny seemed to be giving her the cold shoulder—he'd given her just one quick glance in the hallway but then walked right on past, acting like a big shot with his friends.

If she could have read his thoughts, she would have known that he was actually just bashful, like she was, and also a bit embarrassed at how he'd bungled those few romantic minutes after the party. Not knowing Danny's reason for avoiding her, Julie felt depressed and confused and angry. A few moments later, Julie ran into Lisa in line at the cafeteria. They found a table and sat together while they ate. Lisa was a good listener, and she was still in that contented mood she had been in at the party, so Julie just went ahead and let all her concerns about Danny spill out.

Lisa nodded in a friendly way as she listened, but unlike most of Julie's friends, she didn't try to push her opinion of what Julie should do with Danny. Finally Julie was all done talking, and she definitely felt better, having a friend who really listened.

After a moment with the two of them just sitting without talking, Julie asked, "So you can see, I'm just bumbling through. What's your secret? Don't tell me you're immune to boys and all the rest."

Lisa hesitated, looking off into the distance for a moment. "Oh, I have my bad days," she confessed.

"But you seem to have everything under control, inside you. I envy you—how do you do it?"

"You'll laugh at me," Lisa said.

"No, I won't, I promise."

"Well, I guess I'm just lucky, that's all."

"Lucky? How?"

"My parents, they—I know it's not the hip thing to say you're into, but, well, my parents are really cool. They get along and . . . well, they meditate together, no big thing—and a couple of years

ago I asked them to show me how to do it. They always seemed to feel better after sitting, and well, that's maybe my secret, if I have one."

Julie was a little surprised. "What? You mean like you sit and contemplate your belly button?"

They both laughed. "It's nothing mysterious," Lisa told her. "And it's not a religious thing for me, it's just, well, it keeps me from climbing the walls—most of the time. I do a quick kind of meditation my dad taught me, even at parties and things, to keep at least partway collected."

For a moment Julie didn't say anything in response to this. Her only exposure to meditation had been in movies about the sixties—gurus with robes and beards and all the rest. And then there was her weird uncle who came to visit her father now and then and sat around in his underwear smoking dope and meditating, for hours on end, out in the back garden. "Um," Julie finally said to Lisa, "I don't think anything like that would help me."

"What is it that you want to change in your life?"

"Oh, there're about a thousand things like school and parents and boys and grades and worries and jealousy and all the rest that bugs me but that I can't really do anything about. I'd give anything just to now and then feel like you do, without all this shaky nervousness and getting mad at someone, and all the confusion and worry and, you know, getting depressed. . . ."

"Hey, I'm not immune to all that."

"You look like you are."

"Well, like I said, I guess I'm lucky that I know a way to quiet myself down and let go of upsetting thoughts. What my parents taught me to do when I get upset is this simple shifting in my mind. Like magic, in just a few minutes, like I did at the party, I can usually get away from feeling nervous or angry or whatever and go to a place inside that I really love."

"What? That's what meditation is all about?" Julie asked.

"Well, partly. It's a way to gain control of those thoughts that are bugging you and tell them to just shush up."

"And that's what people are doing when they sit around with their eyes closed for hours on end looking weird?"

"Well, who knows what's weird," Lisa said.

Julie was quiet, thinking about all this. Then she met Lisa's eyes and smiled shyly. "So, is meditation something I can just, you know, learn?"

"It's not hard, really, I could show you. Um, if you want, you can come by my house later this afternoon."

"But I . . . I don't think I can hold still for five minutes, let alone an hour," Julie admitted.

"There's no timing or rules or anything, at least not with what I do," Lisa told her. "You can meditate for two minutes or ten or whatever. Like I said before, I do a little mini-meditation a bunch of times every day, just for a minute or two, especially at school or at a party. Without it, I don't know what I'd do."

"Well, I'm willing to try it. But . . . isn't it boring, just quieting your mind and sitting there?"

"Just the opposite, it's total fun. You never know what's going to come into your mind next. It's like finding a way to sneak up and catch your thoughts doing all sorts of crazy stuff, and then realizing you can change the way your mind works if you want to, so that you stop thinking all those thoughts that bum you out."

Julie reflected on this for a moment, something was not making sense to her. "Well, this may seem like a dumb question, but if meditation works so well to help people feel better, get over anger and anxiety and all that, then how come they don't teach us how to meditate at school?"

Lisa smiled her soft smile. "That's a good question," she said.

"I hate to admit it, but what would Danny think if he found out I was fooling around with something so strange?"

"Well, here's the way I see it: Either he'd think you were strange and you'd know he was a dummy, or he'd want to find out about it, too, and you'd have fun. Like I said, my mom and dad, they really like to meditate together, it's an important part of their relationship."

Julie hesitated, then asked: "Have you ever had a boyfriend, that you, you know, meditated with?"

Lisa blushed just a little. "Oh, sort of. I had a boyfriend back at my last school, and we were beginning to get into things like that. But then, well, we moved."

For the first time, Julie saw upset feelings pass across her new friend's face. Then it was time for next class, and they parted.

~~~~~~~~~~~~~~~~~~~~

Julie, Lisa, and Danny aren't unusual people, but they are about to embark on a most unusual journey as they begin to explore how to take charge of their own minds and feelings—and change their lives in important ways—using a new approach to the ancient tradition of meditation. Although the changes that happen in their lives as they discover new inner powers are sometimes quite remarkable and exciting, these changes aren't at all strange; we can all gain major benefits when we quiet our minds and explore the deeper realms of who we really are.

As you read through this book and enjoy the sometimes traumatic yet ultimately deeply fulfilling story of these three young adults, you'll also be given the time—like we are doing now—to experiment with the meditation techniques that Lisa teaches Julie and Danny. You'll find that, very quickly, you'll be able to get right into the experiences they're having as you take charge of your mind and emotions—and transform your life in directions of your own choosing.

Each time we pause like this to reflect on what's happening with our adventurous meditation heroes, you'll also have the chance to put the book aside for a few moments to actually experience the particular inner process that Lisa is teaching to Julie, and then to Danny and others. In this way, by the time you get to the end of the book, you'll have learned everything they've learned—and you'll be the master of your mind.

Right now, let's start this all off with what Lisa's going to show Julie in the first chapter—a simple but perhaps the most powerful meditation ever, called the "Breath Meditation." Read through the following paragraph and then see what happens when you pause and experiment with the inner mental process.

Without making any effort, experience the change that takes place within when you turn your attention to the physical sensation you're feeling right now of the air flowing in and flowing out of your nose or mouth as you breathe. Just tune into your breathing with all of your mind's power of attention, and watch six breaths come and go . . . and be open to a new experience!

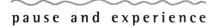

pause and experience

PART ONE
Breath Awareness
(Starting on the Path)

In this first section, we're going to jump right back into our story as Julie visits Lisa and begins to learn what meditation is all about and how it can change her life for the better. Meditation has been around for almost forever—it's at least thousands of years old—and this section sheds beginning light on where it came from.

Along with the personal stories and historic information offered in this section, you'll also begin to learn the most basic and important meditation, that of turning your mind's full attention to the experience of your own breathing. You'll also have a chance to see how parents might respond to the idea that their children are learning how to meditate—and then learn more about the actual inner mental dynamics of how you can use your mind in new ways to experience new realms of your own potential.

At the end of the chapter you'll learn a specific Breath Meditation that will be the foundation of all the other meditations in this book. And you'll discover that you can do this meditation not only when you specifically set aside time for it, but at any time during the day—even right now, as you read these words!

CHAPTER 1
What Is Meditation?

The address Lisa gave Julie was just a few blocks from where Julie lived, and that afternoon she walked over somewhat uncertainly, having definite doubts about whether something as strange as meditation would do her any good. She'd never been able to control her thoughts or feelings before, why should she be able to master something as complicated as meditation? From what she'd picked up here and there in stories and movies, people who meditated were serious disciplinarians, holding themselves in strange contortions in freezing caves for decades before . . . before what?

By the time she got to Lisa's house Julie was certain she'd made a mistake in accepting Lisa's friendly offer. Her mind was back to worrying about its usual concerns, mostly about her parents these days, whom she feared might suddenly spring a divorce on her, and of course there was the whole boyfriend thing with Danny, and the difficulties she was having grasping math and physics. Her dad was an electrical engineer and he demanded his only child to be as brainy as he was, even if she wasn't.

Knocking at Lisa's front door, Julie was half-expecting a hippie crash pad when the door opened, but the living room was a beautifully furnished modern space, clean and roomy and tasteful. Lisa smiled that smile of hers and showed Julie around, introducing her to her mother, who was as normal-looking as Julie's own mom. And when Lisa showed Julie the family meditation room on the second floor, with its spacious windows and comfortable, over-stuffed pillows on a thick natural rug, well, this wasn't strange at all, in fact it was downright cozy.

"So what do I do first, stand on my head?" Julie joked as Lisa sat down cross-legged on one of the pillows.

Lisa had a good sense of humor, and laughed. "Actually, I've never taught anyone about meditation before, this is my first time. So maybe I'm not going to be very good at it," she confessed. "Maybe I should get my mother to talk about it with you, and—"

"No, no. I want to hear how you do it yourself," Julie said.

"Okay then, I'll just do my best. Go ahead and ask whatever questions you have, maybe this will just happen on its own."

"My questions will probably be stupid, I don't know a thing," Julie admitted. "My mom used to take me to Sunday school when I was little, and they tried to teach us to hold still and close our eyes and pray—is meditation the same thing?"

Lisa thought a moment. "Well, from what I understand, when people pray, they're 'talking' to God, there are a lot of thoughts and ideas and beliefs and, well, talk going on in praying. Meditation, the way I understand it, is just the opposite. It's all about quieting that chatter part of the mind. It's a way to let silence come into your head so that you can listen and experience —and just quietly observe what's happening."

"But," said Julie, "what if the main thing happening inside my head is all my nonstop thoughts?"

"I know what you mean. What you do then is just watch those thoughts as they come, and then watch them as they go. Instead of getting caught up in your thoughts, you learn to keep some distance from them and just watch them come and then disappear. You start to get this great feeling that you aren't just your thoughts; you have this deeper observer part of you that can step back and watch all the thoughts go by and quietly maintain its own distance."

From what her parents had told her, Lisa went on, and from books she'd read, meditation shows us that we're much more than just our thoughts and ideas and ego personality. When we learn how to watch our breaths, and at the same time our thoughts, and then encourage the thoughts to become quiet altogether, a seemingly magical thing happens. Our inner awareness suddenly expands and we become intensely involved in the present moment, in the deeper feelings and experiences that are happening right here, right now. Rather than being caught up in just one part of our brain, we suddenly become conscious of everything at once.

"Well, I think that sort of thing has happened to me before," Julie told her. "I mean, sometimes I just space out . . . and suddenly everything's . . . different. But as soon as I notice that something cool is happening, and start thinking about it, it instantly goes away."

"Yes! That's just what I'm talking about," Lisa said. "We all have these moments that happen now and then on their own. What meditation does is let you have that experience whenever you want."

The two girls sat quietly a moment, the flow of words temporarily stilled. Julie realized that very seldom with her other friends did they ever just stop talking altogether. The silence in the meditation room with Lisa was at first a little uncomfortable for Julie, and she almost spoke up to joke about being afraid that silence would sneak up and scare her, or something silly like that. But instead, she noticed that Lisa was watching intently the beam of sunlight coming through the window and filling a small rectangular shaft with thousands of tiny lit-up particles. Julie let herself stare at the sunbeam a moment. Everything seemed perfect right then—the softness of the light, the quiet sighing of the breeze outside, the sensations in her body. . . .

"Probably the main thing that I should tell you about meditation," Lisa was saying, "is that it's all about tuning into your breathing. Just then, were you aware of your breaths coming and going?"

Julie tried to remember. "Um, I think so. I'm not sure."

"When I was little, I remember listening to my parents and their friends talking about breathing, about how meditating on your breathing turns your mind's attention right away toward the center of who you are. I mean, we're alive because we keep on breathing in and breathing out . . . and if we want to really be aware of ourselves, of our own aliveness, if that's a word, then the easiest way to do that is to turn our attention to our breathing. Does that make any sense?"

Julie was quiet a moment. "Well, maybe. Let me try it."

For maybe a dozen breaths they sat together, just breathing. Then Julie broke the silence with her report. "I can feel the tingle in my nose when I inhale," she said softly. "And I do feel more, well, here."

"Hmm."

"And at the same time," Julie went on, "I can feel all the movements in my chest, and in my stomach, as I breathe."

Lisa nodded but didn't say anything. Julie closed her eyes and let her attention tune again into all the sensations that her breathing was naturally causing, and for a few moments she was just sitting there, breathing, and aware of herself breathing. Then a few more moments went by, and a few more. Her breathing relaxed step by step, and a beautiful flush of good feelings came flowing into her. She found herself suddenly aware of her whole body at once, right here in the present moment, and it was such a wonderful experience!

Without warning she popped out of her meditation. A thought had started running through her mind, saying "Hey look, I'm meditating!"

She sat there beaming with a big smile, and she met Lisa's eyes. "I think I just did it!" she said. "I was somewhere else for a minute or two—well, not somewhere else, I was entirely here. I can't quite say it, but I liked it. Can I do it again?"

Lisa just laughed her soft laugh and closed her eyes. Julie felt excited but at the same time a bit concerned about whether she could "do it" again. She closed her eyes, and started to turn her *mind's focus of attention again to whatever she would find happening inside her as she breathed.*

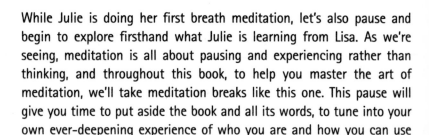

While Julie is doing her first breath meditation, let's also pause and begin to explore firsthand what Julie is learning from Lisa. As we're seeing, meditation is all about pausing and experiencing rather than thinking, and throughout this book, to help you master the art of meditation, we'll take meditation breaks like this one. This pause will give you time to put aside the book and all its words, to tune into your own ever-deepening experience of who you are and how you can use your mind to effortlessly expand your life.

In all the world's meditation traditions, conscious breathing is the key to success. You don't make an effort to do this; you just make the conscious choice to focus your mind on the sensations coming to you as you breathe. The beauty of breath meditation is that there's nothing to do—you're already always breathing. All you do in the meditation is become conscious of what's already happening.

The reason breath meditation is so powerful is because your breath experience is purely happening in the here and now. The sensations coming to your brain are not in the past, nor in the future. Those breath sensations you can feel right now, even as you're reading these words, are utterly in the present moment.

The optimum way to approach breath meditation is to first tune into the sensations you're feeling in your nose or mouth as you breathe. Then you expand your awareness to include the sensations in your chest and belly, while at the same time holding your mind's focus on these two happenings.

Let's do it . . . after reading through the following paragraph, feel free to put the book aside and experiment.

Just sit there and relax . . . and don't make any effort to "do" anything. Just begin to see what happens inside, what experiences and insights come to you, when you turn your mind's attention gently but surely inward—toward the actual sensations you're experiencing in your nose or mouth, and also in your chest and belly, as you inhale . . . and exhale. Feel free now to put the book aside, close your eyes perhaps . . . and tune into your own breath experience for as long as you wish.

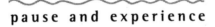

pause and experience

CHAPTER 2

Where Did Meditation Come From?

~~~~~~~~~~~~~~~~~~~~~~~~~~~

Julie is the kind of person who, right away, after she gets interested in something, wants to know all she can about it. So Lisa gathered up several books for Julie to take home and read, books about the early origins and techniques of meditation traditions throughout the world. That night Julie finished her homework as fast as she could, and then spent several hours reading the history of meditation.

She found out that probably the earliest formal meditation tradition came from ancient India where, over four thousand years ago, many thousands of Hindus—mostly men in those days— devoted their entire lives to focusing their attention inward rather than outward, and discovering the universe that lies within.

From those early pioneers of inner-world exploration emerged one of the most enduring meditation traditions of the whole world, usually referred to as yoga. This ancient approach to spiritual awakening included not only specific ways to use the mind to meditate, but also special physical movements and postures that stimulate a deep inner experience.

Julie wondered if Lisa did any physical yoga or "hatha-yoga" as it was called in the book she was reading. Having something physical to do each day that would calm her down seemed a good idea. She also wanted to learn more about the Hindu teacher Patanjali, who, around the time of Jesus, wrote a book called The Yoga Sutras *that seemed to be the main ancient text about meditation.*

After reading a couple of chapters in her yoga book, and having enough information to digest in that area, Julie switched to a book about a meditation tradition that developed almost as far back as yoga. This one came from north of the Himalayan mountains in China. As she read this second book, she learned for the first time about a civilization that spent countless lifetimes practicing its own approach to looking inward and discovering who human beings are from the inside-out. Like the Indian Hindus to the south, the Chinese Taoists had discovered, just by looking inside themselves, many of the same scientific truths she was learning in modern physics, especially about how everything is intertwined into one greater, perhaps infinite, whole of which all of us are a part.

But whereas the Indian yogis of the Hindu tradition were analytical and intellectual in their understanding of the mind and how it works, the Chinese tended to be more intuitive. The Chinese talked about how it is impossible to say anything about what they called the Tao, or the Way, because it is so infinitely greater than man's logical mind.

Regularly in the Chinese Taoist text Julie found quotes from a little book called the Tao Te Ching by an ancient sage whose name was Lao Tzu, and she wondered if Lisa might have that particular book that she could borrow. It seemed to be mostly in poetry form, which she liked very much, with simple yet very powerful sayings like:

In living, be close to the land.
In meditation, go deep in the heart.
In dealing with others, be gentle and kind.
In speech, be true.
In ruling, be competent.
In daily life, be competent.
In action, be aware of the time and the season.

What Julie noticed most in these two books was that the seemingly simple inner act of breath awareness was a primary focus for both of the ancient meditation traditions. Patanjali made awareness and control of the breathing his central focus in meditation, with practical quotes such as "Observing the inhale, the held breath, and the exhale as they occur naturally in space and time, you can learn to make your breathing more harmonious." Lao Tzu likewise, but in his more mystic approach to meditation guidance, asked: "In attuning your breathing to induce tenderness, can you become like a newborn baby?"

The more she read about breathing, the more Julie understood why it was so important—after all, each new breath keeps us alive. At the same time it also demonstrates that we're not separate from the outside world because we're constantly bringing the outside inside us, and then transforming and breathing out that same air. In a chapter on breathing, Julie learned the astounding fact that each and every day, because we all live in the same great planetary ocean of air, we breathe in at least one air molecule that Jesus once breathed. And at least one that Lao Tzu had breathed, and one that Patanjali had breathed. So along with the present-moment importance of breathing, we're also connected intimately with the past through our breathing.

Eager to get more of the overall picture, Julie jumped ahead to her third book, about Buddhism. She'd of course heard about the Buddha, but she didn't really know when he was born or his life story or anything. So she settled into her bedclothes, fluffed her pillow, and started reading about how Buddha's family name was Siddhartha, and that he himself was a devout Hindu, born around 400 B.C. into a rich ruling family in India. Lao Tzu had lived a hundred years earlier, over in China. And Patanjali lived a hundred years or so before Jesus was born. Julie realized that all of these spiritual teachers lived around the same time and all of them came from Asia or the Near East.

Siddhartha was raised in the Hindu tradition of his parents and community, but even though he did his best to find spiritual *awakening in that tradition, somehow that approach didn't quite work for him. He spent six years wandering around India as a Hindu seeker trying to attain enlightenment, which means complete spiritual awareness and liberation. But this approach failed to liberate him from his inner sufferings and confusions. He finally just gave up, let go of all his efforts to push himself into spiritual clarity, and simply went and sat under a big tree. And suddenly, right in the middle of his giving up and just "being" there under that tree, he experienced a radical, totally amazing experience of who he was and what life is all about. In this spontaneous awakening experience he also realized certain primal truths about how to meditate.*

Siddhartha, soon known as Buddha, or "enlightened one," spent the rest of his long life walking throughout his region of India, teaching a very specific set of procedures for waking up spiritually. As Julie was beginning to expect, being aware of one's breathing was a primary meditation technique that Buddha taught, called "Vipassana," and that millions of Buddhists and people of all faiths seeking spiritual awakening continue to practice it around the world.

As Julie read about this simple yet powerful breath meditation, she kept thinking of Lisa. Vipassana meditation was basically what Lisa had taught her that afternoon: to sit quietly in a peaceful place and gently turn your mind's attention toward your breathing experience . . . and every time your mind starts to wander off into thoughts, to bring it back to focusing on your breathing.

Julie was finally getting tired of reading, so she put the book aside, turned off her light, lit a candle beside her bed, and sat there cross-legged (even though Lisa had said you can sit in a chair or even lie down and meditation still works fine). At first, Julie's mind was whirling with all the history she'd just read. But step by step she found that she could encourage her focus of attention to let go of her thoughts and instead tune in to the actual sensations of her breathing, which she did.

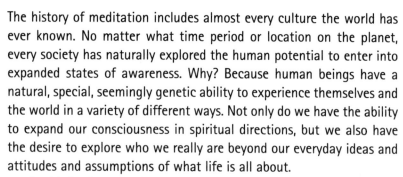

The history of meditation includes almost every culture the world has ever known. No matter what time period or location on the planet, every society has naturally explored the human potential to enter into expanded states of awareness. Why? Because human beings have a natural, special, seemingly genetic ability to experience themselves and the world in a variety of different ways. Not only do we have the ability to expand our consciousness in spiritual directions, but we also have the desire to explore who we really are beyond our everyday ideas and attitudes and assumptions of what life is all about.

In this book, we're focusing on the unified meditation approach of seven great spiritual masters. I'm sure you've noticed that all the different religions of the world—Buddhism, Christianity, Hinduism, Judaism, Islam, and so forth—tend to focus on their differences. In meditation, however, we find just the opposite. All the various meditation traditions of the world, regardless of their differing theologies, approach meditation in basically the same way.

The reason all the meditation traditions are similar at their heart is because all human beings have basically the same brains, and therefore there exists a common neurological process through which we naturally expand our consciousness into deeper spiritual realms.

And the first step for everyone, regardless of cultural differences, is almost always to turn the mind's all-powerful focus of attention directly toward the actual sensations being stimulated in the present moment by our act of breathing. This might seem too simple or mundane a place to approach the divine infinity of our spiritual being, but you'll discover for yourself that the truth is just the opposite. Looking toward your own breathing experience is like opening a door, and the more you look in that direction, the more you discover through that door.

Let's jump right into it: To experience and practice your ability to do this basic meditation just as Julie did, you might enjoy pausing after reading the following paragraph.

To turn your attention inward, close your eyes, if you want to, watch whatever thoughts come whirling through your mind, and, step by gentle step, begin to turn your focus of attention toward your breathing experience right here, right now. Let yourself become a pioneer as you explore your own inner universe, be open to surprises and discoveries. If your emotions are active, just let them be . . . accept them. With each new exhale let the emotions come out. Allow your breathing to calm down as you open to inner relaxation and peace.

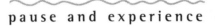

pause and experience

CHAPTER 3

Learning to Find Your Breath

The next morning, even before getting out of bed, Julie got caught up in her usual worries and uncertainties, bracing herself for going downstairs to find out if her parents were still mad at each other. Whenever her mom was upset, Julie was upset, too. And then there was school and a math test, and right in the middle of her first thoughts of the day were her concerns about Danny—would he make her feel nervous or excited or angry or depressed or elated? Well, that morning Julie couldn't even think clearly enough to figure out what was going on between them. She was so shy when it came to boys, and she was beginning to think that maybe Danny was shy, too.

With all these thoughts running through her mind, she got out of bed feeling sick to her stomach and completely drained of any energy to push into the day—until she remembered her new friend and about maybe visiting her again that afternoon. The very thought of Lisa reminded Julie of her breathing, but when she turned her attention in that direction she found a mess of upsetting feelings caught right in the middle of her breathing. And the more she watched her next few breaths the more she felt like crying, so she gave the whole thing up and got into the shower, feeling her usual withdrawn grumps getting the best of her.

Finally, it was last period and the exam Julie had been worrying about all day was being handed out. As she sat in math class, waiting for the exam to start, Julie felt so nervous she could hardly concentrate. Then, from out of the blue, she remembered what she'd read the night before about how tuning into your breathing can calm you down. So she went ahead and gave it a try. She turned her attention to the tense shallow flow of air coming into her lungs, and the weak shaky flow of air coming out of her lungs. At first she didn't like what she found inside, she felt terrible, with those choked-up emotions immediately rising to the surface as soon as she became aware of her breathing.

But on the third inhale something unexpected happened. She felt the hunger for a yawn overtake her, and after a good sigh her whole body relaxed a notch, and her breathing relaxed, too. Her next inhale was actually a pleasure as she took what was probably her first deep breath of the whole day. And when she exhaled, she sighed again, and slumped down in her chair with at least a little good feeling in her heart. As she settled in to do the test, her mind seemed clearer than usual, and she even felt like she got most of the questions right for a change.

She was in a relatively good mood coming out of the exam, and then all of a sudden, right ahead of her, coming along the corridor, was Danny. He was alone this time and so was she, and they both just stopped walking as they reached each other, and looked in each other's eyes a moment.

Then he smiled that smile of his that she liked so much, as if some inner joke was tickling him. "So, how'd the test go?" he asked, because she'd told him it was coming up today.

She was pleased he'd remembered, and she bubbled over with the news that she thought she'd maybe even aced it.

They were silent a moment, uncertain of what to say next, but Julie felt elated, and she noticed that her good feelings were mostly in her breathing, and that each new breath felt delicious. Danny really did like her . . . and she felt like dancing along the corridor.

Just then a couple of guys came walking by and one of them said, under his breath: "Hey, it's dorf-face, the world's greatest Ping-Pong champion."

Danny reacted instantly, muttering something back that made the guy spin around, looking for a fight. Danny was instantly in fight mode, too, fists clenched.

It all happened so fast that Julie felt herself contract in fear—violence of any kind scared her.

"Danny, stop!" she shouted as the other guy pushed Danny on the chest and Danny took a swing at him.

A teacher was walking down the hall toward them, and they backed off and held their tempers so they wouldn't get in trouble at school. The two guys laughed at Danny, then walked off.

Danny was panting with anger when he turned back to Julie. "That guy's gonna get it someday," he growled.

"What's wrong with you? You don't have to fight every punk who says something to you, that's crazy. I don't like it." Julie could feel her breathing totally contract, and Danny was scowling at her like he was mad at her, too.

"Hey," he said, "nobody can control things like that; people push me, I react."

"Well, if you're going to get into fights, you're not going to be a friend of mine, because I don't like that. Please, Danny."

He mumbled something she couldn't understand, still scowling at her.

"Listen, I need to get home," she said, and walked off, feeling ready to cry and scream and pass out, all at the same time.

As she walked down the corridor, Julie did her best to calm her breathing, amazed at how quickly it could shift from good feelings to terrible, and Danny, as he watched her walking away, felt like exploding, too. He was mad that she didn't understand that he couldn't control his anger. And he was mad at himself for not being able to.

Let's pause here a moment and reflect upon the flow of Julie's experiences. As she headed to school she was consumed by all her various worries and concerns—she was nervous, for example, about her test, but then found that she was able to focus her breathing so she could concentrate. This is a major advantage in learning to meditate—being able to calm worried feelings when under pressure.

What about your own experiences at school when you get nervous in class, either taking a test or having to talk in front of the class; do you think you could learn how to tune into your breathing and, in so doing, calm yourself so you perform better? Take time to imagine doing this next time you're nervous at school: Imagine yourself breaking free from your worries by tuning in to the present-moment sensations of your breathing; let your emotions come out and your breathing calm down; imagine becoming more centered and clearer in your mind.

We also saw Julie meeting her boyfriend and, at first, feeling wonderful in her breathing as they opened up and felt their love for each other, but then came Danny's fight, and Julie's reaction as she saw what fear does to one's breathing. It's so important to begin to notice what happens to your breathing when various emotions take over—and also to notice that you can begin to use your breathing to change how you're feeling inside. Again, the trick is in becoming more conscious and experiencing how expanded consciousness helps to soothe your emotions and even transform them.

Notice, for instance, how your breathing feels while you're reading this book; become more aware of your breathing. In fact, there's no situation where you can't be aware of your breathing. And always, when you turn your attention to your breathing, your consciousness begins to expand, your emotions begin to heal and feel better, and you improve your moment-to-moment experience.

Go ahead and do this right now. Let's experiment with something that can change your whole experience of reading this book and learning to meditate. First of all, notice that as you read the words across this line of the page right now, that your attention is mostly focused on taking in the meaning of the words I'm writing, as you process the ideas being talked about. Reading usually tends to take over all of our attention, but it doesn't have to. Instead, even while you're reading these words, you can at the same time expand your awareness and tune into your breathing.

Give it a try; keep on reading, but also begin to feel the sensation of the air flowing in and out of your nose or mouth as you breathe . . . it's easy actually. All you need to do is to make the choice to include your breathing in your awareness, no matter what else you're doing. In this way, while you're reading this book, or any book, you can also be meditating on your breathing!

This is called "meditation in action" and is just as important as spending time each day sitting and doing nothing else but meditating. So, you now know that you can be doing one thing, like reading, and at the same time be aware of the air flowing in and out your nose as you breathe—and also the movements in your chest and belly as you inhale and exhale. It's that easy; all it requires is remembering to choose to expand your awareness to include your breathing in whatever else you're doing.

And now, let's pause completely from reading and just do pure breath meditation for a while. Like any other ability, the more you practice, the better you get at it, which is why we're pausing so often to let you practice more and more.

So, after reading the following paragraph, take a break.

Put the book aside, close your eyes if you want to, and begin to open to the present-moment experience with each new inhale, and exhale. Let your breathing stop when it wants to . . . and start again when it wants to. Set your breathing free and see where it leads you.

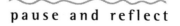

pause and reflect

CHAPTER 4

What Will Your Parents Think?

When Julie got home from school she was still upset about what happened with Danny. She went into the kitchen to grab a snack and found her mother sitting alone, staring out the window. Julie poured herself some orange juice and sat down. Her mom said nothing.

Not liking the silence, and typical of her usual bluntness, Julie just came right out and said, "So, Mom, what do you know about meditation?"

Her mother looked up at her a moment, came back into the present with her feelings, and sighed. "Oh, meditation," she said. "Why would you ask a question like that?"

"No reason, just curious."

"Well, actually," her mother began, shifting into a more positive mood, "when I was in college my roommate Teresa was a meditator; she'd just hold in her mind some simple Sanskrit words that she would say over and over, for half an hour every evening."

"And did it make her feel better, to meditate?" Julie pressed on.

"Feel better? Oh, well, I guess it did. I remember she was a nice girl, and she loved her meditation time, she tried never to miss it. But I didn't try it, the whole thing was so beyond me. She had her guru in his white robe, Maharishi I think he was called, he came to the campus once—thousands of people went to hear him. Teresa . . . I wonder what happened to her?"

"So if meditating makes people feel better," Julie said without hesitation, "maybe you should try it. You're certainly grumpy most of the time these days."

Her mother just shrugged her shoulders and stared a moment, reflecting on some inner thoughts she didn't express to her daughter. Julie waited as usual for some communication, but her mom wasn't much of a communicator these days, except when she got mad and started shouting.

"Anyway," Julie said lightly as she got up, "I'm learning."

"Learning what?"

"To meditate," Julie said almost in defiance, and headed back out the door to go to Lisa's house.

A man in a business suit answered the door at Lisa's house and welcomed her in, saying that Lisa would be back home in a few minutes. He led her into the living room, explaining that he was home from work early that day. "So, you're the girl who walked away with all our meditation books," he said with a smile, sitting down on the sofa with her.

"Oh, I'll be finished with them tomorrow," she promised.

"No hurry with those books, we've all read them, take your time. Besides, you don't really learn to meditate just from reading books, the real proof's on the inside, as I'm sure Lisa has told you."

Julie was trying to imagine this totally normal businessman sitting down every day and meditating. "Lisa says you meditate every day," she said.

"Well, now and then I miss a day, but I do my best."

"I was just wondering," she said to him with her usual upfrontness, "what made someone like you decide to learn? Did you meet some guru when you were in college or something?"

Robert laughed. "Nothing that exotic," he said. "Way back when I was starting my first job, my health fell apart because of all the stress, or so my doctor told me. Anyway, rather than giving me antianxiety medication, he was hip enough to suggest that first I try meditation to calm me down. At first I thought the idea was dumb, but I went to see a psychologist he recommended and learned meditation from her. She taught meditation as a psychological process, so I don't do any particular religious kind of meditation, just what works best for me."

"But somebody did teach you."

"Well, she got me started with the basics, breathing and whole-body awareness and a few verbal cues. Then as Ruth and I got more into it, we read a bunch of books and went to a couple of weekend seminars on meditation. We found a routine that we loved, and we just kept doing it. Be careful, I'm warning you, it's addictive."

"Is that bad?"

"Just the opposite. If you make meditating a habit, it can change everything for the better. We're even giving people at work ten minutes twice a day, if they want, to take time to meditate. The scientific evidence is getting steadily more solid that meditation at work helps clear the mind, open up good communication, spark insights, and reduce stress. I'm glad Lisa's showing you what she knows—the earlier the better. Sorry to leave you but I need to change for tennis. See you later, okay?"

Lisa arrived home a few minutes later, and after grabbing a snack from the kitchen for both of them, she led Julie out into the backyard because the weather was great that day.

"Your dad's cool," Julie said as they walked across the lawn and settled down into a breezy spot in the sunlight. "I'm still expecting people who meditate to be hippies and fanatics of some kind, not businessmen."

"Well, my dad's just another normal adult. That's why, when I was growing up, I assumed regular normal adults all meditated. It wasn't until I was seven or eight and talking with my friends at school that I started to find out that other parents didn't necessarily stop every day and calm down with meditation."

"My mom sure would do better if she would learn," Julie said. *"Well, maybe if you do, she will, too."*

～～～～～～～～～

Let's pause for a moment so you can reflect on Julie's experience as it relates to your own. First of all, we saw her wanting to talk with her mother about meditation. Have you ever talked with your parents about what it means to learn how to look within, to get to know yourself better through meditation? What do you think your parents' opinion of meditation and the spiritual path in general would be?

Some of you will have parents who are very positive about meditation, and who might even want to learn how to meditate with you. Perhaps they'd be receptive to a birthday gift of a meditation book, or even would want to learn from you. But of course, some of you will have parents who think meditation is dumb, or too esoteric, or contrary to their religious beliefs.

If your parents are unsupportive of your new interest, carefully listen to their reasons, and then do your best to explain that, no, you're not getting involved with some weird cult and, no you're not going to run off to an ashram. Instead, you're learning a form of meditation that is psychological, not religious, that it doesn't violate anybody's religious beliefs because it's not about beliefs at all, it's simply about becoming more aware of reality.

Luckily, we're living through a period of history where meditation even appears on the covers of major magazines, and is being lauded as a wonderful way to reduce stress, overcome anxiety, and improve mental functioning. So the world around you will also be helping to tune your parents into the positive results of learning to meditate.

Most important, your own evolution into a brighter, more emotionally balanced, happier person will speak for itself. As you "let your little light shine," people around you will see that the effects of meditation are considerable and excellent.

On the slight chance that your parents can't get beyond thinking that meditation goes against their religious beliefs, you can simply stop talking about meditating and simply do it. As we're learning, each and every moment of the day, you can be in meditation gear by simply being aware of your breathing and expanding your consciousness, no matter what you're doing. And no one else needs to know what you're doing in your own private universe.

Some people have parents who are just great. Others have parents who are less than great, whose emotions and attitudes are hostile, judgmental, fearful, and otherwise bothersome to be around. You'll find that as you become better and better at watching your breathing and holding your own inner calm, you don't have to react so much to your parents if they're in a down mood. You can gain through meditation a sense of emotional distance from people who are aggressive or depressed.

This is a great power to attain—that of choosing not to react to the negative emotions of other people, parents or otherwise. There's such freedom to be experienced in learning that you don't have to be a victim of other people's reactions. Julie is just beginning to learn that when Danny gets upset or aggressive, for instance, she can maintain her own inner calm and not get sucked into his reactive habits.

Do you think you can learn to become master of your own emotions? Pause a few breaths, look to your breathing and emotions right now, and notice how the focusing of your mind's attention to your breathing changes your breathing in expansive ways.

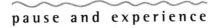

pause and experience

How Does Meditation Work?

Julie and Lisa were sitting outside in Lisa's backyard, enjoying the gentle air and getting ready to start their meditation session.

"I read a lot about more advanced techniques in those books you loaned me," Julie said. "Will you maybe teach me some more techniques today?"

Lisa smiled. "Hold on, not so fast," Lisa told her, but not in a pushy way. "The thing about meditation, at least how I understand it, is that you don't get better by learning more and more techniques. There're a thousand variations on the same basic themes, and my mom says a lot of people get so caught up trying to learn all sorts of complicated techniques that they never settle into one of them long enough to really discover what it's all about."

"I think I already know what it's all about," Julie said enthusiastically. "I did the breath awareness last night, and even in math class today, and both times something good happened, inside me."

Lisa smiled. "That's great," she said. "You're lucky. Sometimes at first nothing much happens and people get impatient, or you start thinking that meditating is dumb and a waste of time. That's what happened with my boyfriend back where I used to live."

"Oh?"

Lisa almost said something more, but then just shrugged her shoulders.

"So," Julie went on after a quiet time, "I watch my breathing, like Buddha. Is that all I should do?"

Lisa was quiet a moment. "Well, remember, I'm not a medi-

tation teacher. All I can tell you is what works for me, from what I learned from my parents and from reading books, and recently being in some online meditation chat rooms and so forth. But I know this without any question: It's the breathing that's most important because all the other techniques build on breath awareness. If you can start making a habit of pausing and watching your breathing every time you have a few minutes free, that's the most important thing. For me, when I'm not aware of my breathing, I'm really not very aware of myself at all, I'm just running around on automatic pilot with my thoughts all over the place. But as soon as I remember to tune into my breathing, things get better. It's amazing, all sorts of feelings and experiences open up that would otherwise go right by."

She stopped talking, and rather than thinking of something to say back to her, Julie just went ahead and did what they'd been talking about: Right then and there she tuned into her own breathing.

After about an hour, Julie followed Lisa into the house, having just spent a very interesting time watching her breathing and also watching the birds and clouds and butterflies flying by. This was the new meditation that Lisa had chosen to show her—being aware of your breathing and at the same time being visually aware of things around you.

The experience had been curiously engrossing for Julie because it was effortless to do, it enabled her to stay enjoyably in the present moment for quite some time, and that time passed with her hardly noticing it. She'd simply held her mind's focus on two sensory happenings at the same time—breathing and seeing —and just doing that basic perceptual meditation had shifted her feelings in wonderful directions.

Lisa had done the meditation with her, and several times when they suddenly found themselves looking at each other, they'd burst out laughing. Then one time their eyes had met and they hadn't laughed, they had just looked into each other's eyes for quite a while without any smiling at all . . . until Julie had looked away somewhat bashfully, feeling as if she had almost seen right into her new friend's soul.

Now they were heading into the kitchen for something to drink after being in the sun so long, and Lisa's mother, Ruth, was making dinner, whistling softly to herself as she cut carrots and dropped them into a big soup pot. The smell of the soup in the air was good, and Julie found herself still doing a bit of the meditation, watching her breaths and smelling the soup at the same time.

"Mom," Lisa said, "Julie asked me something I don't know the answer to."

Ruth stopped cutting carrots. "Oh, what's that?"

Lisa told her Julie's question about how meditation actually works in the brain, what's happening inside that makes the whole world suddenly change in a subtle but definite way when the mind's attention shifts from one thing to another. The question as Lisa tried to express it came out long and a bit confusing, and Ruth stood a moment, reflecting.

"Well, I'd guess it'll take me at least five minutes to even make a start on that question," she said to Julie. "And to be honest, science doesn't know many of the meditation answers yet. But I was reading a book recently that I don't think Lisa has read yet, called *Why God Won't Go Away*, with the rather scary subtitle of 'Brain Science and the Biology of Belief.' It's actually a good book, discussing new experiments done on the brains of people while they're meditating. From what I understand so far, it seems that the key step in meditation is the act of deciding to shift the mind's focus away from its usual fixations—on ideas and thoughts and images and so forth—and toward a totally different function of the brain, one of perceiving something in the present moment."

"You mean, like perceiving our breathing?" Julie put in.

"Exactly, or watching a candle as the Hindus often do, or contemplating nature like the Taoists do, or reading scripture verse like Christians are taught to. The important thing is shifting the brain's electrochemical activity from one part of the brain to another part of the brain—a shift toward observing actual happenings in the real world rather than being lost in our own thoughts. It's the shift from cognition to perception, if you know those words."

"We're studying all that in biology," Julie said.

Ruth nodded toward a shelf. "Why don't you two raid that cookie jar," she suggested, and as the two girls munched cookies she explained how the human brain is actually made up of four separate brains in the same head, each with distinctive jobs and capabilities.

First there's the left hemisphere of the brain that does most of our thinking and analyzing and judging and so forth, using symbols to make rational thoughts and decisions. This part of the brain is always focused on a particular point, moving from one thought or idea or fixation to the next in a linear progression. This is the part of the brain that is active in reading and making sense of the words you're reading right now.

Then there's the right hemisphere of the brain; this does the primary work of perception, of experiencing the real world directly through the senses. This region of the brain has the peculiar ability to "see everything at once" rather than always being focused on a point. That's why the right hemisphere of the brain is associated with intuition and flashes of sudden realization and "knowing." It's also been shown in brain scans to light up when a person is observed while meditating. As the thinking, judgmental left hemisphere becomes less active in meditation, the right hemisphere becomes more active.

There's also the older (evolutionary-wise) limbic part of the brain, found down below the two cerebral hemispheres, where our emotions are said to live. Brain research has recently shown that our emotions are usually stimulated not by what we perceive in the outside world but by the brain's reaction to what we see. This means that our emotions are strongly linked to the thoughts we think, to our prevailing attitudes and judgments, and especially to our ingrained core beliefs about who we are and what life is all about.

One area of this general part of the limbic brain is of special importance in meditation. This is the section that determines whether we are caught up in worries and apprehensions (and therefore unable to really meditate) or whether we are free from agitation and therefore able to quiet down and enter into an expanded state of consciousness. This small but important realm of the brain is called the "amygdala," or the primitive fear center. When we're thinking worried thoughts that upset the fear center of the brain, the peace and calm and clarity of meditation just doesn't happen. Rather, the fear center fires off orders to our various glands to secrete fight-or-flight hormones that make us tense, nervous, and in general uncool. This is why learning to quiet the mind is so important in meditation as well as in life in general.

Finally, down below, even deeper in the brain, we come to the even older "reptilian" brain stem that developed way back before there were any mammals on the earth, but which is still a vital part of all forms of life. The brain stem doesn't think, it doesn't react with any feelings other than fear and well-being; it can't plan for the future or remember the past. Its primary job from birth to death is to regulate the vast complexity of our physical bodies so that our internal plumbing works well.

"When we meditate," Ruth explained, seeing that her young listeners were starting to tire from all the medical details, "what really happens is we tune into the entire brain at once, rather than being stuck in just one particular function of the mind. The reason that tuning into the breathing is so instantly powerful is because the breathing is automatically run by the brain stem, which makes sure we keep breathing enough to fulfill our need for oxygen. Unfortunately, our breathing is also directly affected by our emotions—as I'm sure you've noticed when you get angry, or depressed, or afraid—and those feelings are instantly felt in the breathing, right?"

"Definitely," both girls mumbled at the same time. "And good feelings, too," Julie put in.

"Absolutely," Ruth replied. "And when we meditate, when we decide to be consciously aware of our breathing, we bring our conscious minds into direct encounter with our usually unconscious core brain, so that we very physically become aware of our own selves in the present moment. And in this basic act, we expand our consciousness. Do it yourselves now. Feel your awareness expand to include your whole body as you tune into the sensation of the air flowing in and out of your nose . . . and expand to include the movements in your chest and belly as you breathe—don't make any effort to breathe. Now allow your breathing to stop at the bottom of your next exhale. Experience firsthand that inner spark that makes you breathe your next breath, that keeps you breathing, even when you make no effort to breathe—that's the core of your brain, that's the real you, in a very real sense."

This primal breath meditation that looks to the spark that ignites your next breath is important for us to do regularly. It makes us aware of the source of our aliveness. So go ahead and let Ruth guide you into a direct encounter with this life force that keeps you breathing and therefore living, each and every moment of your life. . .

Just tune into the sensation of the air flowing in and out of your nose and expand your awareness to include the movements in your chest and belly as you breathe. Allow your breathing to stop at the bottom of your next exhale—make no effort to inhale—and experience firsthand that inner spark that makes you breathe your next breath, that keeps you breathing—that's the core of your brain, that's the real you, in a very real sense.

Go ahead and do this "spark of life" breathing exercise several times. On each new breath become empty of air. Make no effort to breathe, experience the inner power that sustains you, become conscious of your physical core of being, get to know it well so that you can more and more trust your inner source of life and learn to live consciously from that power center.

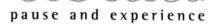

pause and experience

"The brain is so complex, we're just beginning to understand it," Ruth went on after the two girls had paused and looked to their own breathing for a few breaths. *"But when we meditate, it's clear that what we do is choose to take control of how our minds work, rather than being victims of our genetic programming or our childhood experiences or parental and cultural assumptions. We tune into our whole selves in the present moment, and in that act, we wake up to the fact that life is vastly more than what we usually experience. By directing our minds in conscious ways, we become more, well, conscious."*

"But it seems," Julie said uncertainly, *"that when we meditate, we turn our attention away from all our thoughts and beliefs and so forth—away from everything that makes us human rather than lizards or frogs. When we turn our attention away from thoughts to our breathing, aren't we regressing way back to a time when animals were hardly conscious at all."*

"Hmm," Ruth said, and turned to her daughter. *"What do you think, Lisa?"*

Lisa was quiet a moment. *"I guess I wouldn't judge who's more conscious, some politician shouting slogans on TV or a dog with one eye watching the TV and the other eye paying attention to what's happening in the room. What I like about shifting my attention to my breathing is that I pop out of my mind's worries and imagination into the present moment, which is where every-thing comes alive. I agree that being more conscious seems to be what meditation is all about, and when I'm aware of my breathing and my body, that seems a lot more conscious than when I'm lost* in thought. I feel really here, so I can enjoy life—like we felt outside just now, remember?" she said to Julie.

Julie was reflective, and she just nodded. Ruth turned and stirred her soup and then chopped carrots for a moment. Lisa bent down and stroked the big tabby cat that had just walked into the kitchen. Julie was beginning to love these times when her new friends stopped talking and let silence fill the air, silence that wasn't depressing at all. This was new to her; she was used to people sitting around moping like her mother did so often, or otherwise talking all the time they were together, feeling uncomfortable when conversation stopped.

Now, every time there was a pause in the talking, Julie realized it was a chance to tune into her breathing again. She inhaled and, spontaneously, right in the middle of her breathing, a thought came into her mind. She did her best to speak her thought while still watching her breathing.

"I guess I always assumed that spiritual things were totally different from biology and science," she said. "But now that I think about it, it's obvious that we experience everything through our brains—even our spiritual experiences happen right in the middle of our biological bodies. So what's the difference between spiritual and scientific if it's our material brains that do the spiritual experiencing?"

"I've thought about that a lot," Lisa put in, "about how the scientists are now saying it's just an illusion to see things as separate, that it's all one integrated universe. I read this great quote from Einstein, where somebody asked him what caused something, and he said, 'Everything causes everything.' That's the same thing Lao Tzu says in his ancient book, that the Tao is everything, and we're part of that everything, and actually there's no separating us from everything."

"That's just it," Ruth said, "and sometime in school I hope you'll study intensely the actual process of perception, because meditation is all about watching and understanding from the inside-out: how we perceive, how we experience ourselves and the world around us. There's a truly great book I want to loan you sometime, Julie, by a spiritual teacher who lived until just recently, Krishnamurti. He's my favorite spiritual teacher, and he says: 'The first step is the last step in meditation—to uncondition the mind by becoming aware, by becoming totally attentive.' That's it right there: to be attentive, to give your full attention to whatever you're perceiving in the present moment."

Everyone was silent for a while. The cat stretched, then turned and walked out of the room, with all three pairs of eyes watching him. "In cognitive psychology," Ruth said quietly, "they're finding out that, in the brain, you can't separate the thing you're looking at and your own inner experience of it. It takes both your brain and the object, the cat for instance, to create the experience of the object. It seems pretty strange, but logically we don't even exist at all if we take away our environment. The inner and the outer are a seamless whole. There isn't really any separating ourselves from the world around us—and that's where science is proving what the ancient masters found out in their meditations. Like Lao Tzu and Krishnamurti and all the other spiritual teachers say: Each of us is an integral part of the whole. We are all truly one. That's the giant realization that science is just now making that the yogis discovered from just watching their own brains at work from the inside-out."

Ruth looked from one girl to the other, and smiled, realizing that she'd overloaded them with these big ideas. She grinned. "Now off with you, enough thinking, how about some experiencing."

Lisa jumped up, her body tired of sitting, ready for action. The girls thanked Ruth for chatting with them, and then went running outside together.

When we look to see who we really are as human beings, we find that we are first and foremost perceivers. Right now, if you eliminated all of your perceptions, your senses, who would you be? Yes, you would still have your memories of the past, and you would be able to think thoughts about your past, but without your sensory experiences in the present moment you'd entirely lose touch with the present moment, you just wouldn't "be here."

We take our constant flood of perceptions almost entirely for granted most of the time, and actually don't pay most of them any attention at all, especially when we're lost in thought. Meditation is the process whereby we choose to make our perceptions most important. By focusing keenly on our immediate sensory inputs, we in turn awaken a direct encounter with the world around us, with our own inner feelings—and ultimately with our more subtle perception of our deeper spiritual awareness of the presence of our Creator.

So the seemingly simple act of turning your mind's attention away from thoughts about the past and the future, toward sensations coming to you in this present moment, is not so simple. It's in fact ultimate. If you want to feel alive, if you want to be responsive to the world around you, if you want to know what it really means to be a human being, just tune in.

Right now, again, what are you aware of while you are reading these words? You're aware of what you're seeing on this page and also what is in your peripheral vision; you're aware of what's around you in the room. You're also aware (if you expand your consciousness) of sounds. There's never total silence except in a vacuum, so you're always hearing something. And when you combine sights and sounds into an integrated experience, your awareness pops into an expanded state.

And at the same time, you're receiving an assortment of smells. Each new inhale brings an intimate encounter with the scent of everything around you, and there's always a taste in your mouth. And furthermore, there are always myriad of sensations coming from your body's contact with the world around you, as you touch and are touched. And if that's still not enough to be aware of at the same time, there are all the sensations being generated inside your own body, such as your heart beating, your blood pulsing through your veins, your stomach digesting your last meal and so forth and so on.

So, when I say tune in to your breathing, I'm pointing your mind's attention to the first primary sensation that's always happening. And as you tune into your breathing, the mind will naturally expand its experience in sensory directions to include more and more of what's happening in and around you, right now. And suddenly here you are, totally aware, entirely here, fully conscious—in a word, you are meditating.

MEDITATION ONE
The Breath Meditation

We've now explored several different variations on how to approach the basic meditation of tuning into the actual experience of your breathing and your whole body, vitally alive here in this eternal present moment. To end this first part, let's do the formal breath meditation that you'll be using throughout this book. We will expand this meditation in several ways later on. You'll want to begin mastering this basic meditation, memorize it, learn it by heart, and make it your own.

Once you've taken the time to master the process, you'll find you can tap into its power wherever you might be—at home, at school, on a date, while playing sports, or in some unique situation that demands your full attention and capacity. This primary consciousness-expansion meditation can be your ever-trusty lifeline to rapid empowerment, compassion, wisdom, and insight.

Just make yourself comfortable however you want to. Be sure to stretch and move all you want as you find a good posture for the meditation. Go ahead and yawn if that feels good, and allow your eyes to close when they want to.

Now begin to gently become aware of your breathing, turn your mind's attention to the actual sensations of the air flowing in and flowing out of your nose or mouth as you take your next few breaths.

And as you stay aware of the air flowing in and out of your nose or mouth, expand your awareness to include the movements in your chest and belly as you breathe.

Become aware of all the sensations and movements of breathing—in your nose, your mouth, your chest, your belly.

If you feel any emotional pressure inside, accept it, and with every exhale allow that pressure to flow out of you as your emotions become calmer.

Make no effort to breathe; just let your breaths come and go on naturally. After your next exhale, let your breathing stop altogether, until your inner spark of life begins your next inhale, then exhale and stop breathing again; let your inner spark bring in your next breath, tune into the very center of your breathing experience.

And just relax, feel the air flowing in and out of your nose or mouth, the movements in your chest and belly as you breathe . . . expand your awareness to include your heart, right in the middle of your breathing. Experience your heart and your breathing together.

And say to yourself: "I'm here, breathing."

And as your breaths come and go, allow your awareness to expand to include your whole body, here in this present moment; and allow your inner experience to expand and move freely. Be open to a new experience.

pause and experience

To listen to an audio version of this meditation, and the others in this book, please go to www.johnselby.com.

PART TWO
Heart Awareness
(Dealing with Emotions)

This section is going to be all about learning to tune into your heart at the center of your being, and how to deal with whatever emotions you find there. Meditation can be a gigantic help with all things emotional, and the key to learning to manage emotions successfully lies first of all in not judging the emotions you find inside you. When you turn to your breathing, and look to your heart—and experience firsthand your emotional condition at the time—your challenge is to accept rather than reject your feelings. Meditation involves coming to love yourself and accepting yourself more and more as you realize that you're perfectly okay just as you are.

All the various human emotions are expressed through breathing; we can't really separate our feelings from our breathing. So the more you tune into your breathing, the more you'll be in touch with your feelings. And as we'll see step by step, the more you remember to be aware of your breathing, the more you'll be able to accept and let go of emotions that bother you and encourage the ones you like.

Once you begin to employ meditation to heal old heartbreaks and let go of negative attitudes and moods, you'll find that your emotions naturally become calmer, and you'll have the space to regularly enjoy peace of mind and the bliss that emerges when disturbing emotions are soothed. Soon you'll be able to tune into your heart, and instead of confronting upsetting feelings inside you, you'll discover that you feel much better now inside your own skin.

So welcome the feelings you find right in the middle of your breathing whatever they are; breathe into them, let them come out. And as you continue to watch your breathing, you'll see how those feelings spontaneously begin to change . . . for the better!

CHAPTER 7

Opening to Feelings

Danny woke up from a bad dream. He had dreamt that an enraged monster was chasing him through strange streets, breathing down his neck, clawing at his back. He woke up gasping for air, sweating, not knowing where he was.

But he was just in his own bedroom—there was no one after him. He lay there regaining his calm as best he could, trying to get rid of the dream's vivid images by thinking ahead to the coming day at school. Almost immediately Julie was there in his mind— with her sweet, accepting smile, lips that drove him crazy, her whole body, her whole being. Then he remembered how upset she'd gotten with him because he'd almost gotten into a fight with that jerk, and he tensed at the very idea of having to face her. He knew he had to do something about his temper, or he was going to lose her, but what could he do? He should have phoned her when he got home last night to apologize, but his dad had been partying with his new girlfriend, and he'd shouted at Danny for some dumb thing and they'd argued, and he'd just gone to bed and forgotten.

Dressed and heading downstairs, he could hear his dad and the new woman talking in the master bedroom. He went on into the kitchen to grab something for breakfast. He didn't want to see them together. He was still angry at his dad for what had happened with his mom, over a year ago now, so he headed right out of the house with just an apple, munching it as if biting at the whole world. Everything had gone wrong since his mom moved out of the house. Danny had lived with her for a while, but the new school had bothered him, so he'd moved back with his dad. Now he was about ready to move back upstate to his mom's again, but he didn't really want to change schools yet another time—and besides, Julie was here.

Danny had two things that he was really good at. He was the top player on the local Pong-Pong team, something positive that he'd learned from his father. And he liked school. So he plunged into his first class that day with a vengeance. He suspected that most of the guys in his classes were down on him because he was always acing tests, which made them look like dummies, but he didn't care—he'd never needed a lot of friends, anyway. He'd been moved from school to school four times now, and he'd given up trying to have close buddies. People respected him because he was smart, and that was good enough for him.

"Um, Julie?" he said, seeing her ahead of him in the hallway and hurrying up beside her.

She just kept walking. "What?" she said.

"Hey, I'm sorry; he just bugged me."

"You didn't have to explode like that," she told him, still walking, hardly looking at him at all. "I don't like violence, I told you that. Anger scares me."

"So you're just like all the rest, expecting me to be in total control of my emotions all the time. I can't do that."

She walked a few more steps without saying anything, then came to a stop. They were outside now, by the lawn. She turned her beautiful eyes right on him, and he could see she had tears in them. "I don't expect anything," she muttered. "But I have my feelings, too. If you're going to get into fights, I'm going to leave."

"Sometimes people bug me, that's all," he said.

"You're a bomb just looking for an excuse to go off."

"Maybe I am, maybe I'm not—you don't know me."

"That's for sure, you hide like crazy."

"If I'm so terrible, why do you go out with me?" he fired back at her.

She was quiet again for a moment, eyeing him. "Obviously you have other sides to you that I like. And I get angry, too, Danny. I know how it feels. But I don't hit people. When you get violent like that I'm afraid sometime you might hit me, too."

"Get serious," he said, but then he remembered how his dad had hit his mom. "Well, anyway, I'm sorry," he told her honestly. "And I'll try, really, not to let it happen again."

"All you need to do," she told him, "is take a deep breath, not react—and walk away from trouble. I won't think you're chicken. I'll respect you for it, more than you'd think."

"Thanks. I'll do my best. Like I told you a few days ago, things aren't so good at home with my dad. I know I get angry because of it, at least that's what the counselor tells me."

"My parents are always at each other's throats, too. It's so dumb."

"Somehow when I'm with you," he told her honestly, "like right now, everything calms down, I feel better inside. Listen, I don't have Ping-Pong practice today, how about we go for a walk or something this afternoon?"

"I still don't understand why you didn't let me come to your competition last weekend."

He hesitated. "I don't know. I hate to lose when somebody I like is watching."

"Well, you can get over that. Besides, you said you were doing really well on the team."

"It's a wimp sport," he blurted out. "What's it matter if I win or lose, it's not basketball or football or—"

"Ah, so that's it!" she said. "Oh boy, are you messed up."

She meant it lightly, but he reacted. "Well, forget you!" he said to her, and turned to walk away.

She ran after him and pulled him to a stop. "I didn't mean that the way you took it. Stop this. You don't have to explode every time."

"It's obvious I am messed up. I don't know why you hang out with me."

She stood there, emotional, too, her heart pounding and her breathing coming fast. Just then she remembered about her breathing and let her attention go there. Her heart suddenly had this big explosive feeling as she started speaking: "So maybe I can love somebody just the way he is," she said. "Maybe I don't need a basketball star, maybe I just need you."

He stood staring at her, touched to the quick by her words. And right in public she went up on her toes and kissed him quick on the lips. "So there," she muttered, and walked away along the path.

This time it was him coming after her and pulling her to a stop. They looked into each other's eyes. She could feel her breath coming and going and it felt suddenly expansive, delicious.

"So how about it, let's get an ice cream or something later on," he said.

"I can't."

"Oh?"

"I'm seeing someone."

"Oh."

"It's my girlfriend. Hey, why don't you come along with me?"

"Are you kidding?"

"I mean it, you'd like her."

"So what are you going to do?"

She grinned and said right at him, "Meditate."

"Get serious."

"What, you chicken?"

~~~~~~~~~~

Danny is obviously struggling with his feelings, partly because of his tense situation at home with his father, and partly because, well, we all have tempers that can flare up, and we're all learning to control them. Danny is, just like Julie says, a walking time bomb just looking for an excuse to explode. Fortunately, one of the great gifts of meditation is that it allows us regularly to look to our hearts to discover if we're under emotional pressure, and if we are, then right then and there, in a safe place, we can let the emotion out.

How can we do this? First of all, by being honest with ourselves and accepting our emotions, whatever they are. When we try to deny that we're angry even though we are, we make the situation a hundred times more difficult to resolve. And the same applies to feelings of heartbreak, depression, and guilt. First of all, we need to look inward to our heart, to our bodies in general, and get honest with ourselves. "I'm angry!" "I'm depressed right now." "I'm so worried I can hardly breathe."

Both Danny and Julie are struggling to be honest, not only with themselves but with each other. Julie is already beginning to be aware of her breathing while talking with her boyfriend, and it's helping her to open up and be honest. Hopefully Danny will be interested in learning how to do this as well.

How about you? Do you have a temper? Are you going around with a broken heart but not letting your self accept what happened, feel the hurt, and let it go? Right now, see what happens when you pause for just a few moments (or of course longer if you want) and go through the ritual.

Tune into the breath sensations in your nose. Expand your awareness to include the movements in your chest and belly as you breathe. Right in the middle of your breathing notice how your heart is feeling and see if you can breathe into this feeling even if it hurts. Accept how you feel right now.

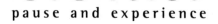

p a u s e   a n d   e x p e r i e n c e

CHAPTER 8
Healing Heartbreaks

When Lisa got home after school she found a note from her mother that Richard, her old boyfriend, had phoned. He hadn't called for so long, she'd thought he'd deserted her altogether even though they'd promised to stay together somehow—even with the hundred miles between them now.

Her heart started pounding in anticipation of hearing his voice as she ran upstairs to her bedroom, sat down on her bed, and dialed his number. He was the first boy she really had given her heart to, and she was breathless when she heard his voice on the other end of the line.

"Richard, hi," she muttered. "It's me."

"Oh, Lisa, hi."

"Long time no hear," she told him. "I was wondering."

"Well," he said, "things are real busy here, the team and all. And there's something I need to tell you."

Lisa's breath froze. "Oh. Uh, what?"

"It's just that, you know, we're so far away, and well, this is hard to say, you know I like you and all, and always will, but you remember Deborah."

"Uh, Deborah . . ."

"Well, we've been seeing a lot of each other, and I thought it's only fair to tell you that we're going together now. It was just a natural thing. I hope you understand."

Tears welled up in Lisa's eyes. "Oh, I see."

"Please, Lisa, don't be upset. It wasn't going to work out anyway, what with us being so far apart; we both knew that. You probably have some new guy you're hanging out with, too, right?"

She sat there ready to burst out crying. She didn't want to act so dumb over the phone, so she just hung it up. There was nothing more to say anyway.

She did cry after hanging up the phone, there was no stopping it. Finally, though, the tears subsided and left her just sitting there, limp and empty. Her breathing was so shallow that regularly she exhaled and then was motionless, inert, some part of her feeling dead and gone, but then the next inhale would come on its own, as if telling her that no matter how she felt, life goes on. Some distant part of her took note of how she was responding to heartbreak, observing dispassionately what happens when you're rejected by someone you love. But most of her was so caught up in the aching pain in her heart that all she could do was throw herself down on her bed and let more tears flow.

Her mother noticed right away that something was wrong, and took Lisa out to sit on the back porch. They just sat together, not saying much after Lisa described the phone call. Ruth knew enough not to try to make her feel good when she was feeling rotten. All she said was, "Life hits us hard now and then. There's no avoiding it. Just do what you can to stay in your heart and let it heal. You've lost a friend, but you still have your best friend: yourself. And me. We'll see you through."

Lisa went back into the house and up to her room. Her emotions were a mess and so she turned her attention to her breathing and her heart—and almost immediately she felt a rush of aggression when she thought of Richard being with another girl, kissing her and touching her and doing everything with her. It made Lisa so angry that she found herself ready to scream—and she actually did. She went ahead and just screamed bloody murder at him, over and over. Then she calmed down and let her breathing begin to recover . . . that had felt so good!

Suddenly her door popped open and there stood her mother, upset. "Lisa, what on earth's happening?" she asked.

Lisa found herself smiling. "Oh, nothing, Mom, I'm just meditating like you taught me."

Let's discuss what we just saw. For instance, we saw Lisa, supposedly our great teacher of meditation, having difficulties with her own feelings. Like anybody else, she feels vulnerable in romantic situations, and she's just had her heart broken. So meditator or not, she has a lot of upsetting feelings to deal with. We saw her alone in her bedroom, and instead of entering into beatific peace she explodes with angry shouts as she releases her emotions.

Here's a question: Does it change your notion about meditation to realize that sometimes, instead of inducing peace, meditation can induce a violent emotional release of things like anger? And does it scare you to think that when you meditate, you might tap into upsetting feelings rather than getting free from them?

Of course, the good news is that meditation not only puts us in touch with whatever feelings have been building up inside us, the meditation process of focusing on our breathing and our hearts encourages us to release those emotions—and thereby heal them. A basic law of emotional healing is that if we honestly express an emotion when it arises, that emotion is beautiful and healthy and trustworthy. It's only when we stop expressing our emotions that they build up, get distorted, and come out in unwanted and sometimes harmful ways.

Hopefully this chapter's honest exploration of the emotional dimension of meditation will encourage you to want to meditate regularly, so that you can keep your emotions healthy and quickly released, rather than pent-up and therefore upsetting.

CHAPTER 9

Moving through Emotions

Lisa was surprised but not upset when Julie arrived half an hour later with Danny for their afternoon get-together. She was feeling better, and the sight of her friend helped boost her feelings at least temporarily. "I've seen you at school," she told Danny as he stood a bit sheepishly in her living room. "Didn't you win that Ping-Pong tournament a couple of weeks ago?"

He shrugged his shoulders. "Uh, yeah," he said. "That was me, for what it was worth."

"So have you played Ping-Pong with Julie?" she asked him, glancing at Julie. "She told me she has a table in her basement."

"No, she hadn't told me about that," he said, also looking Julie's way. "Look, I don't want to barge in on your afternoon."

"Just the opposite, you're more than welcome," Lisa said. "We're just going to go upstairs and talk and things. Julie's curious about meditation, and I know a little. Do you want to join us?"

He shrugged his shoulders again and grinned. "Why not? I'm no Buddha, but I've got a navel somewhere."

So upstairs they went, and into the cozy room with rugs and pillows and a wonderful view of the woods. "Where's the incense and candles?" Danny joked, and Lisa brought out both. "Sometimes they actually do help," she said.

"Well, maybe you two can hold still in some yoga pose for half an hour, but I know I can't," Danny said, feeling uncertain. "Maybe you should just do whatever you do and I'll come back when you're done."

"Danny, please, it's no big thing, don't leave," Julie encouraged him. "What I was thinking was, maybe Lisa would tell

us about something I read in a book last night, about how meditation gives people control of their emotions." She turned to Lisa, who was already sitting cross-legged on a pillow. "Danny's like me," she told her. "We both sometimes get angry and blow up. I thought you might tell us what meditation has to do with things like that."

"Hmm," Lisa said, as the other two sat down. She looked from one to the other. "Maybe my dad might know more about anger."

"Your dad meditates?" Danny asked.

"Half an hour most mornings, and another half an hour some evenings. And mini-meditations all through the day, so he says, at work. He used to have a lot of aggression inside him, that's mostly gone, thank God."

"Sometimes," Julie said, "when my mom and dad argue, I get more and more uptight until I just want to smash things and scream at them. But I hold it in—and feel miserable, depressed. So what can meditation do for me when I feel that way, anything at all?"

Lisa met her eyes, and Julie noticed for the first time that Lisa didn't look her usual bright self. "I remember something," Lisa said, "that my mom told me that maybe relates. She said all of our upsetting emotions start with particular thoughts we're thinking, that anger, for instance, doesn't just spring into existence on its own. It always gets fired up by what we're thinking, about someone, or some situation."

"No," Danny said. "It seems like just suddenly, without any thoughts at all, I'm ready to explode, like yesterday in the hallway when this guy pushed me and called me something. I was instantly ready to hit him. Julie was there, she saw it."

"Well, tell me exactly what happened. You were feeling good, just minding your own business."

"Yeah, exactly, but then this guy I know from English class, this real dork baseball jock, called me something."

"Dorf-face," Julie said, remembering.

"Okay, so right at that moment, when he called you that, some idea must have sprung to mind, you must have had some particular thought."

"Well sure," Danny admitted, remembering. "I mean, first of all, I thought he's going to ruin my time with Julie and that made me mad, and then I thought, he's insulting me. And right away there was this pressure inside me because of something my dad said to me recently. When this guy pushed me, the thought went through my head, 'Hey, you push me again, I'll hit you!' and that was just what I'd thought when my dad pushed me."

"Whew, that's a lot of thoughts at once," Lisa said.

"And right as they went through my head, I was charged to fight. Julie here, she's telling me that I should somehow be able to block that reaction and just stay cool. But by doing what?"

Danny was breathing hard, caught up in his emotions.

"Well, what I hear," Lisa said, "is that you're under emotional stress in general, and you're holding angry feelings locked up inside you."

"Damn right. If I fight back against my dad, he clobbers me. He outweighs me by sixty pounds and he's a carpenter, a real fighter. You don't just meditate your way out of a fight with that guy."

"I'm not saying that meditation is some magical solution," Lisa said, a bit defensively. "All I know is that whenever I take the time to stop and watch my breathing and find out what emotions are under pressure inside me, they begin to ease up, the pressure goes down. Meditation may help you in general to let go of the anger that's inside you, so that you're not under so much pressure."

"Hey, I've tried to get rid of it," he said honestly, "but it doesn't just go away. Instead it comes exploding out at the wrong people."

"Well, let's try an experiment," Lisa proposed. "I'll show you a meditation my mom showed me, for helping my pent-up feelings dissolve and be gone. Shall we?"

"Uh, whatever," Danny said.

"I don't see you as someone with a lot of pent-up emotions," Julie put in.

"Oh, are you kidding? You can't even see what I've been through today?"

"Well, I did notice something. Is there something . . ."

Lisa hesitated, took a deep breath. "Oh, just my old boyfriend from my other school phoned and said we were through. I've mostly expected it, but it hurts anyway, you know."

"So what did you do, meditate it away?" Danny asked.

Lisa sat there not saying anything for a moment, then shrugged her shoulders. "It's still inside me, but yeah, after I cried I was able to just live with the pain, feel it, and you know, after a while it got better. Meditation doesn't do miracles, but it helps."

"So what should we do, what's the first thing?" Danny asked.

"Well, first of all, you just do what we're doing, which is deciding to take a certain amount of time, say five minutes or so, and not do anything else, not answer the phone or jump up because you remember something that needs doing. Just decide to take five minutes off."

"All right, done that," Danny said.

"Maybe we should begin with what Julie's already learning," Lisa suggested. "Just set aside the next minute or two to do nothing except watching your breaths come and go, not as an idea about watching your breathing but actually feeling the sensation of the air flowing in and out through your nose or your mouth. Let your attention focus more and more on how you keep breathing, even when you make no effort to breathe. Just set your breathing free and watch as it keeps right on happening."

Lisa was quiet for a while, and the three of them sat there doing nothing at all, just breathing without any effort, their attention tuned into whatever sensations came to their bodies.

"And now," Lisa said quietly, "you can also be aware, at the same time, of the movements in your chest and belly as you breathe. Feel your heart beating right in the middle of your breathing; expand your awareness to include your head, your feet, your hands, your whole body at once—right here.

"Relax your tongue, your jaw, and without judging, begin to notice any emotions you find, perhaps under pressure, inside your chest. Keep your attention on your breathing, and your heart, and just open up to whatever feelings are there. Don't think about them, just be aware of their pressure and presence, inside you."

Again she fell silent. Julie glanced at Danny and noticed that his eyes had closed. She watched him sitting there, and she felt a rush of feelings in her heart for him—it was pleasure, but with a subtle edge of tense uncertainty, and definitely excitement.

She closed her own eyes and watched her own feelings and her breathing, and with every breath she noticed changes. She could feel the pressure inside her slowly becoming less edgy, less tense. As her breathing slowed, her emotions seemed to calm down, too, until suddenly, as she watched her breaths come and go, she was effortlessly aware of her whole body at once, from head to toe. And her body seemed filled with a soft feeling of plain old simple love and oneness with Danny, and with Lisa as well.

But Danny wasn't having such an easy time inside. This was serious for him because, with each breath, he could feel his anger increasing rather than getting reduced. With his eyes closed, he kept watching that pressure building, and thoughts kept rushing through his mind even though he didn't want them, random memories of the last argument he'd had with his dad and what he wished he'd said to him but hadn't.

His eyes popped open and he saw both girls, who were being so kind to him, and he thought of his mother, and instead of the anger he suddenly found himself choking up in his throat. He held his breath, afraid to let those feelings come out in front of everybody. Lisa had said to stay aware of his heart, but he found so much pain there that he couldn't stand it, and even though he tried to stop them, tears welled up in his eyes.

He closed them, wiped his eyes with the back of his hand, breathed through the mouth a few times to calm down, and surprisingly found that this tiny release of his emotions had relieved something inside him. His breathing was changing, softening; he was actually feeling better for having let some of those bad feelings come out.

He felt restless now, unable to just sit there with his eyes closed. He found himself looking over at Julie, just breathing and looking at the same time, and the sight of her changed the feeling again in his heart and in his breathing. He felt as if he could almost inhale her presence with each breath, and that felt strange but really good. He closed his eyes again, and this time when he dared to turn his mind's attention to his heart, he found his heart felt softer. With Julie's image still in his mind, he sat there actually feeling good inside. His breaths were coming and going until the thought popped into his head that this was all ridiculous, that meditating was for sissies. He'd never be able to hold on to a girl as wonderful as Julie, that as soon as she met his dad it would all be over because his dad would probably be rude or even make a pass at her.

His eyes popped open and he realized his breathing was tense again, and at the same time he noticed that both girls were looking at him. They seemed so relaxed and contented, while he knew he was all tense.

"Uh," he said uncertainly. "Five minutes up?"

"That was about ten minutes," Lisa said. "So how did it go? How do you feel inside now?"

"Oh, uh, I don't know. I ran into a lot of emotions. Then it got good for a while. Then a whole lot of thoughts came that made me tense." He was quiet a couple of breaths, then said: "But yeah, I guess I liked it. I'm surprised. I'd never done anything like that before. But the emotions, I didn't know what to do with them, they wouldn't just calm down and go away."

"I know, mine were pretty wild today, too," Lisa admitted. "My mom and dad just let their emotions come right up and out sometimes when they meditate, it seems freaky at first to see your dad with tears in his eyes, but they say it's healing to let the emotions flow, even though we're all uptight about it. I do it, too, sometimes, and it's always good when I set my breathing free and the pressure is relieved—then I feel better."

"So that's what meditation is, this emotional thing?" Danny asked.

"That's the first step," Lisa said. "To just look and see what's going on inside, and to let the feelings come up and out with the breathing and be gone. Then, that's when you can go on into the deeper stuff."

"Emotions are plenty deep enough for me," Danny admitted.

Julie felt a little laugh starting to well up inside her, one that she couldn't keep quiet.

"Now what is that?" Danny asked defensively, thinking she was laughing at him.

"Nothing, I just realized why people tend to go off and meditate in private—so nobody sees their emotions coming out."

"Well, okay, I'll tell you," Danny admitted, "at one point I actually thought I was going to break down and cry like some dumb baby right in front of you. That would have been totally embarrassing."

"Well, I'll probably be the first one to do that," Lisa told him. "I've got this big cry inside me still. But here's the thing, like my mom always says: We all have these feelings inside us, so why are we so embarrassed to show them, especially considering it always feels good to get the feelings out and gone."

"I wouldn't know," Danny said. "I mean, when I've cried, like when Mom left, that wasn't a good feeling at all."

He stopped talking and looked down at his hands in his lap, feeling emotions welling inside him that he didn't want to show anyone.

He felt Julie's hand take his. He looked up into her eyes. He sniffed. She smiled just slightly. "When my parents argue, I usually end up in my bedroom with the door locked, crying," she said, her own eyes shining with emotion.

They sat there a moment, not saying anything.

"Well, this was just an experiment," Lisa said at last. "And I'd say it went well, at least we got a taste of this part of meditation. And that's just a beginning, there are all sorts of different experiences, different ways you can look inside and discover things."

"Well, this was good, thanks," Danny said. "I sure didn't expect the afternoon to go like this."

"Me neither," Julie said, and without any hesitation at all, leaned over and gave him a hug.

Let's pause a few moments here and consider what just happened with Danny. His experience was unexpectedly intense, and meditation can sometimes get that way. After all, it's an exploration into what we really feel, and when we open up to what's real inside us, we have to be honest about what we find. Meditation is all about being honest, surrendering to what's real.

What about you? When you turn your attention inward, to your breathing, and your heart, do you feel any emotions under pressure inside? Sometimes there's more pressure inside than at other times, and sometimes you'll find yourself already at peace with no emotions to release at all. Meditation always helps you take your emotional temperature, and then do something about it if you're under pressure.

One of the reasons so many people are learning how to meditate these days is because meditation offers one of the very best ways to safely discover what emotions are under pressure inside you, and then let them blow off at the beginning of each meditation session. This initial step in meditation encourages your whole mind and body to let go, to be free to explore the deeper realms of who you are, what emotions are begging for attention and release, and what you're capable of in life.

Please hold in mind that we're engaged in a long-term exploration here, and not expecting instant results or changes. Danny tapped into his feelings a bit, and with each time he pauses to meditate, he'll continue with the emotional healing process. But this takes time for most people. So you can relax and rest assured that as the days and weeks and months go by and you begin to include more and more meditation in your life, whatever emotions plague you will begin to lighten, to let go, and dissolve.

So just take your time with this big issue of tuning into your heart, and releasing and healing pent-up emotions while meditating. We'll be talking about this process over and over throughout this book. For now, if you want to, you can pause and let yourself get more accustomed to the general process of turning to look to your heart; after all, practice makes perfect.

Get comfortable. Stretch and move until you find a balanced way to sit, or lie down if that works better for you, and gently begin to turn your mind's attention to your breathing. Notice if your breathing is smooth and calm or uneven and tense and just accept whatever you find: the sensation of the air flowing in and out, the movements in your chest and belly as you breathe, and the feelings in your heart. Open up to them, let them be there, and with every exhale let the pressure come flowing out.

pause and experience

CHAPTER 10

Understanding Your Feelings

After their meditation, conversation had drifted off to school things.

"Oh, it's getting late," Julie finally said, looking at her watch, "I need to head home for dinner." She stood up and looked over to Danny.

"Me too," he said. "So what do you two do, get together and meditate like this every day?"

Lisa looked to Julie, then to Danny. "We just started a few days ago. Where I lived before, a few of us got together on Sunday mornings, you know, to have our own kind of spiritual get-together. It was fun. But mostly since we moved here, I just come home and meditate half an hour or so in the afternoons, to regroup after school. And Julie's been coming by. Future's wide open."

"Well, it's interesting, I'll say that for it. You got any books I can read on meditation?"

Julie laughed. "I stole all their meditation books yesterday," she said. "You can borrow a couple of them if you want to come by."

Julie felt proud to be walking down the street for the first time holding hands with a boyfriend like Danny. Something had happened between them up in Lisa's room, she knew that, and she liked it. But as she got closer to her own house, she felt more and more nervous—and she could see, like Lisa said, that it was thoughts springing into her mind that were making her feel anxious. What if her parents didn't like Danny? What if they were arguing and embarrassed her the first time she dared to bring Danny by?

Her mind was full of worried thoughts that did nothing but upset her. So she tried to shift her mind away from her thoughts and toward, well, Lisa had said to shift to something in the present moment. So Julie let her attention focus on the feeling of Danny's hand in hers, and the soft scent in the air from somebody's fireplace, and the sound of birds singing nearby. And suddenly she found that her full attention was here and now, her worries silenced, and her breathing, well, just coming and going as she watched, and there was her heart right in the middle of her breathing, singing along with the birds.

She was able to stay in this state of mind where everything was okay until she got within sight of her own house and saw that her father's car was in the driveway. He was home, and who could say what the atmosphere might be inside. She went up to the front door, nervous again, but there was no need to be. Her mother was talking with a friend on the phone, and her father seemed in a good mood, shaking hands with Danny without getting one of those judgmental expressions on his face.

"Danny's a champion Ping-Pong player," Julie said spontaneously.

"Ah, then he's got a match to play downstairs before he leaves this house," her dad said, grinning. "I consider myself a bit of a champ, too, Dan—at least I used to be in college. Nothing serious you know, just kids banging balls. How about a game in, oh, half an hour or so?"

"Uh, sure," Danny said.

Her bedroom was up the stairs and way down the hall and she felt a funny rush of excitement as she lead Danny off into her personal space. When they got inside and she closed the door and he just stood there looking around, she knew he'd think she was immature with her old posters on the wall and her childhood dolls over on her dresser.

"Mm, cool," he said. "My room's such a mess, you wouldn't dare walk into it."

"Here are the books on meditation that Lisa loaned me, take your pick," she said, handing him the books.

He sat down on her bed and opened the first one—one that she'd already read partway into. "I never thought I'd be reading books on meditation, I tell you," he said.

"Me either," she agreed.

"I'll start with this one if you don't want it right now," he said, and handed the others back, and just like that he started reading the book. For a moment Julie sat there just watching him, really feeling his presence in her room. Then she took one of the other books on meditation, and sat down in her comfortable chair across the room from him.

"Um, you want any music?" she asked him.

He glanced up at her absent-mindedly, already into the book. "Music? Uh, no, not unless you do."

He looked back down to his book and she started reading, too, just opening the book in the middle, most of her attention still on the boy here in her bedroom with her. For a couple of paragraphs she read without even processing the words, but then she started paying more attention and found herself reading about how some people with high blood pressure could get it back down to normal just by learning how to meditate. There were also studies showing how, after surgery, people who regularly calmed themselves and focused on simple healing meditations recovered faster than people who didn't do anything like that.

"Listen to this," Danny spoke up, "it says here that you can't feel love, and feel fear, at the same time. Is that right?"

She glanced up. "Hmm, I never thought about that."

"They've done studies; it's some psychological fact: The fear response in the body, shifting into fight-or-flight readiness, getting tense and afraid of getting hurt, it's the opposite body condition *that you feel when you feel love, where you're trusting, relaxed, open, and whatever."*

He fell silent, looking across into Julie's eyes.

"Love's a pretty big word," she said. "But it's true: If I'm afraid of you, like I said, I wouldn't be able to love you."

"That's why Mom left Dad, bottom line," he admitted.

"Jeez. Harsh."

"Oh, Dad has his good days; he's not all bad. But he just explodes without any reason sometimes."

"That's terrible," she said, almost inaudibly.

"Well, you don't get to pick who your parents are. Now my mom's gone off the deep end with her born-again stuff, just the opposite of Dad. It's no wonder they couldn't make it together."

"I have to warn you," she said, "my parents get after each other, too; it can get pretty upsetting around here all of a sudden. But I do love them. So I guess, except when I'm angry at them or afraid, yeah, I love them."

They looked at each other, then at the same time, both of them looked back into their books. Danny started reading about how the primary inner freedom we have is the freedom of where to direct our focus of attention—toward something that upsets us, or something that makes us feel good. Well, he thought, what about when my dad is throwing one of his anger fits—there's not much choice of focusing on something enjoyable then. But then again, he thought to himself, except when he's on a rampage, which is like ten percent of the time max, maybe I don't have to be going around fuming about him so much . . . that's my choice.

"Here's something interesting," Julie was saying. "Buddha laid out four Noble Truths that are supposed to sum up the entire situation for human beings. First of all, until we learn how to control our thoughts, we're always going to be caught up in suffering emotionally—there's no escape. The second Noble Truth says we suffer not because of the things around us but because of

our thoughts about our situation—all our judgments and worries and so forth, like Lisa was saying. Our attitudes and beliefs and all our negative programming from childhood, they're what keep us locked in our inner torture chamber."

She paused, looked off through the window, lost for a moment in her own reflections about whether this was really true. Danny sat there watching her, thinking that when he's with her, it's the opposite of a torture chamber. She turned her head suddenly and caught him watching her—and she blushed.

"So what's the third Noble Truth?" he asked. "The first two sound pretty depressing."

"Ah, the next one is better. It says that we all have the ability to wake up to our own Buddha nature, that we can expand our consciousness and really live in the here and now, free from our worries and depressions and everything that our own thoughts make us wallow around in."

"Hmm. Well, if meditation can do that for somebody, then it's for me. But I keep thinking, if it is such a giant help for people, then why doesn't everybody do it?"

"I read in one of those other books last night," she said, "that we have to make a big step, our ego has to let go its king-of-the-mountain attitude in order for us to be free from suffering. And people are afraid to let go like that, to surrender to something greater than their ego."

"Ego. I don't even know what that really means," he said. "I mean, what would we be without an ego, isn't that the part of us that runs the show, that makes sure we take care of ourselves and do what we need to do?"

"I'm not sure," she said. "But obviously something keeps people from just easing up and getting along and not fighting. Look at the world, everywhere there's people hating other pcople, tribes and countries and all the rest. And what I was reading, about love and fear, is that unless we really look right at our fears, which cause all our hatreds and aggressions and all the rest, unless we look right at what we're really afraid of, there's always going to be violence in the world."

They were both quiet for a moment. That had been a bigger idea than either of them could quite swallow. "So, what's the fourth Noble Truth of Buddha?" he asked her finally.

She looked back down to her book and read a couple moments, then looked back up. "Just what Lisa was saying, that there is a definite logical set of steps we can take inside our minds to wake up and expand our experience so that we're no longer caught in fear and ignorance. And I guess that's what meditation does."

"I always thought," Danny told her, "that meditation was something only adults did, and just the weird ones at that. I never thought kids could meditate. I don't mean that we're kids, but adults don't consider us grown-ups. All this that I'm reading, it's aimed at adults, not us."

"Who cares," Julie retorted. "Why should they get the goods and keep us away from them?"

"Well, maybe meditating is dangerous," he said.

"Lisa looks okay to me."

"She's great, isn't she," he commented without thinking.

Julie glanced suddenly at him. "What?"

He noticed her reaction. "Hey, I didn't mean that. She's just a cool person."

Julie sat there a moment, feeling flushed, and realized she had suddenly felt afraid of losing her boyfriend to her girlfriend. She noticed her breathing and it was tense, shallow. As she watched it, and saw the kindness in Danny's eyes toward her, almost immediately the tension let go and she found herself almost laughing.

"What's so funny?" Danny retorted.

She looked him right in the eye. "I was clobbered with fear and knocked right out of love for a minute," she explained, drawing on what they'd been talking about earlier. "And it was just like they say in the books: Some thought I let run through my mind about you and Lisa made me feel just terrible."

"Well, I won't go around her anymore, if that makes you—"

"Danny!"

"What?"

"That's the whole point."

"What whole point?"

"That I don't have to go off into negative fantasies about what might happen. I mean, I don't own you, and I'm not going to go around afraid that somebody is going to steal you away from me. Maybe somebody will, but aren't we learning right here that it's just plain dumb to spend all our time afraid something might happen in the future? I don't want to do that with you."

He slowly took in her rush of words. "Uh, okay then. I'll admit. From the time I first set eyes on you I've been afraid that some guy, somebody more popular or more handsome or something, would end up being with you instead of me. It's been a torture. And you're saying I should just give all that worry up?"

They stared at each other, both of them feeling something new, something deep, for each other.

Suddenly there was a loud knock on her door and they both jumped.

"Hey, Danny, how about that Ping-Pong?" her father was shouting.

Julie glanced at Danny—he was holding his breath like he'd been caught doing something wrong—and they both burst out laughing at the same time. He grinned and gave her a quick kiss right on the lips, then he stood up and walked over to the door.

"Ping-Pong? Great idea," he said.

We've just moved through loads of ideas about meditation and spiritual awakening without taking a breather. Let's let Danny go down and see how he fares in Ping-Pong against the father of the girl who's completely won his heart while we take just a few moments so that you can look to your inner feelings about what we're exploring.

We also saw that Julie is beginning more and more to notice when her breathing is getting tense and her emotions uptight. Walking with Danny, she caught herself thinking ahead to what might happen at her house, but then she applied what she's been learning and brought her focus back to the present moment, where everything was entirely enjoyable, walking hand in hand with Danny.

In your own life, you can do this more and more, too. All you have to do is pay attention to when the pressure of your emotions is starting to build inside you, and also to notice what thoughts are causing that buildup. Then, as you become good at the various meditations of this book, you'll learn how to take charge of your mind and shift your focus of attention in directions that make you feel good rather than bad.

We all tend to be afraid of losing someone we love, and the stronger the love, often the stronger the fear—in the form of jealousy and chronic worrying. Julie finds herself with the beginning twinges of jealousy that Danny might leave her for Lisa, but then she catches herself thinking these thoughts, honestly talks about them with Danny, and moves through them. This is a basic process you can also use to avoid a lot of the agonies that otherwise accompany romance.

Meditation is often thought of as a purely solitary thing, but we're seeing that there's also great value in learning to meditate with a friend . . . so we can talk about what we're learning and exploring, and let our ideas steadily grow by sharing them. Right now you're reading a book about learning to meditate. You might want to begin to reflect upon whether you'd like to share what you're learning with a friend.

Buddha talked about the four Noble Truths, as we just heard.

1. Life is suffering for us as long as we remain unaware of our deeper nature beyond our ego's materialistic plottings and chronic worries;

2. We suffer mostly because of our negative and fear-based thoughts;

3. We have the potential to move beyond all our programmed confusions and apprehensions; and

4. Meditational tools are available to help us to make that move into inner freedom.

For the next few minutes, or for however long you want, from one breath to a hundred, while you put aside this book and watch your breathing here in the present moment, let your mind reflect upon your own readiness to honestly look inward to discover who you really are. And then go ahead and see what happens when, with every new breath, you just continue to hold your mind's focus of steadily inward as you look to your heart to see who you really are.

pause and reflect

CHAPTER 11

Dealing with Your Parents

Danny was surprised at how tough a fight Julie's dad (who'd told him "Hey, just call me Peter, nothing formal here") put up against him. Danny won the first game, Peter the second, and Danny the third—and then Julie's mom appeared in the basement doorway asking Danny if he'd like to stay for dinner.

The idea made him tense; he'd have to phone his father, which he did from the basement phone, but got no answer. He left a message about his dinner plans and then went upstairs, answering Peter's questions about the way high school Ping-Pong tournaments were conducted these days.

Dinner was about the best Danny had had in a long time, probably since his last dinner with his mom. He answered questions from these friendly parents but felt shy at the same time, wondering what they thought about him being friends with their daughter. And she was about the same, eating and glancing at him but mostly going mum.

"So what are the books you're carrying around?" Peter asked him after a lull in the conversation, as Julie and her mom served dessert.

"Oh, I just borrowed them from Julie," he explained.

"Schoolwork?"

"Uh, no—just some books on how the mind works and that kind of thing. Meditation and so on."

Peter eyed him a moment. "Julie has books on meditation? That's a new one," he said, not hostile, just surprised.

"Well, it's an interesting topic," Danny said, winging it a bit.

"I'm usually caught up in all sorts of busy buzz in my head, maybe meditation can calm me down a bit."

Julie had come into the room. "Don't let Dad get on one of his rampages about religion," she said. "He considers himself a recovering Mormon. But Dad, meditation isn't a religion at all."

"Hey, I know that," he said.

"What?" Julie reacted.

"I know the difference between religion and meditation, meditation comes from the East, where they don't have a giant concept of a condemning God the Father, right? There's no God at all in meditation."

"That's not quite right," Julie's mom put in, having sat back down at the table with everyone digging into ice cream banana splits. "I took a course in comparative religions back in college, and as I remember, the Hindus had an entire pantheon of gods, like the Greeks did. There was Shiva, and, um—I forget, but they were gods."

"Maybe that's Hindus, but not meditation," Peter said, his voice rising slightly in argument. "Meditation doesn't get involved in beliefs at all, it's pure looking without thinking, directly experiencing with no priests in the middle to tell you want you're supposed to experience."

"But it's not a godless practice, Peter. You make it sound like—"

"I was only saying that—"

"Mom! Dad!" Julie said, upset. "Stop it, do you have to argue about meditation, too? Neither of you even do it . . . or you wouldn't be so impatient with each other in the first place."

Julie's parents were temporarily silenced, glancing at each other, while Danny looked down at his ice cream intently.

"I only meant," Peter said, calmer, "that I read a couple of books a long time ago about meditation, like Danny is here, and I remember liking how you don't have to take on any religious belief system in order to do it."

"So, did you try meditating?" Julie asked him.

He shrugged his shoulders. "Yeah, a little bit. But it didn't work for me; my thoughts kept my mind so full that I couldn't get into any sort of inner peace doing it. That's not to say I didn't like it, I'm glad you're looking into it, Julie, really. Don't let my failure dampen your interest."

"Oh, I won't," Julie said back to him, almost defiantly. "And maybe you didn't have a good teacher like we do."

"What, a teacher? You found a meditation teacher in this town? I didn't know they let gurus within the city limits," he joked.

"Actually," Danny put in, "it's a friend of Julie's, this girl whose parents have been meditating for about a thousand years, so she knows how to do it in a way that, I don't know, seems to make sense. I'm just reading these books to find out where meditation came from. Lisa's already taught us the basics. It's not hard at all."

"It was for me," Peter admitted. "I liked everything I read, but I just couldn't sit still for more than a few minutes without getting antsy. But don't let me discourage you. Hey, Danny, do you like jazz?"

"Peter," Julie's mom said impatiently, "why'd you change the subject like that, why can't you—"

"Mom, there you go again," Julie said, afraid they'd launch into another argument.

"I only brought up jazz," Peter said, "because I have this great CD called Music for Zen Meditation. When I listen to that album, that's the closest I've come to meditating. It's from the sixties, recorded in Japan just impromptu. I think Alan Watts, the well-known Western Zen Buddhist, went over there and helped get it recorded; it has one of the old American clarinet jazz greats, Tony Scott, playing just total improv with these two traditional Japanese musicians, and it came out, like, just totally beautiful.

You want to hear it?"

Danny was done with his ice cream and said sure. He went into the living room with Peter, a little uncertain about whether he should have offered to help with the dishes. But Julie came with them and they sat around and listened to some definitely great quiet jazz with a low wooden flute and a twangy Oriental string instrument Peter called a "koto."

"For me," Peter said, "listening to music is the closest I get to meditating. I can get caught up in all the various instruments, listening to them all at once, and my mind suddenly gets entirely quiet. I guess that's why I love jazz, it can take me off like that."

"I was reading," Julie put in, sitting right next to Danny on the rug in front of the big speakers, "that meditation works psychologically because you turn your mind's attention away from your usual thoughts, toward your breathing, your heartbeat, and sometimes another sensation like sounds, or something you see. And when you hold your attention to two or more sensory things at the same time, just automatically the thoughts stop flowing through your mind. It's some psychological law, you can't think when you're attention is focused on two present-moment perceptions at the same time. Danny, you have the book now that talks about all that."

"Well that makes sense," Peter said enthusiastically, "because right now I'm hearing the music, and I'm listening to you at the same time . . . and there're no thoughts. Sometimes I listen to Bach to calm down and it's the same basic principle, it's called 'contrapuntal music,' where there's two different melody lines going at the same time. When I really listen, I shift almost right away into a calmer place in my head. Probably music in general makes people like it, regardless of the type, because of what you just explained. See, I learn something new every day, and even from you kids," he said, and because he said it in a real friendly way, Danny took it that way.

Before Danny left that evening, Peter burned him a copy of the CD on his super-fast CD burner so Danny could take it home. Julie walked outside with him and they went down the street a little way, holding hands as if it was entirely natural for them. They stopped under a big tree, and didn't say anything for a while.

"Well," Danny said finally, "that was an unexpected turn of events today. Thanks, for everything."

"I guess we should thank Lisa," she said.

"Hey, thank Lisa, thank you, thank your mom, and definitely thank your dad. He's cool; you're lucky to have a father like him."

"Oh, I guess so," she said hesitantly.

"I know so."

"Well, the good news is he likes you, too," she said. "If you're not careful he'll get you down to the basement every day after work, he needs somebody who can stand up to him down there, that was great."

"Mm. Well, I'd better go," he said, tensing a bit. "Who knows what my dad will be up to."

"Is he really that bad?"

"Oh, the counselor says I need to understand him, that he had his own father who was even worse with him, so he's naturally that way. But damn it all, I don't want to end up that way, too."

"Don't worry, Danny, you won't. I know. You're . . . wonderful."

She went up on her tiptoes and kissed him on the lips, and they came close and lingered longer than they had before, then she bashfully let go, turned, and went running back to her house.

~~~~~~~~~~~~~

As we've discussed in earlier chapters, everybody's got their own particular family situation to deal with; it seems that no parents are perfect. So as we grow up, all of us have to deal with the bad as well as the good in our home situation. What we're learning here is that we don't have to remain locked up in the emotional habits and tensions that come from our families. We have the choice, and the freedom, to begin to notice how we react with our parents, our brothers and sisters and so forth. And then, we have the inner power to begin to change our more negative reactions so that we break out of the emotional habits that upset us.

One thing we're seeing, as we follow Danny and Julie and Lisa around in their everyday lives, is that parents are also capable of learning and waking up and changing their habits. And sometimes their own children can bring in new ideas and ways of acting that, in turn, begin to affect the parents. Julie is just starting to have new insights as to why her parents seem to always fight, and her parents at the same time seem open to maybe learning how to break out of their argument routine.

The reason meditation is such a great tool for helping resolve negative family situations is because at least one person in the family, the one who's learning to meditate, will begin to calm down and stop reacting blindly and habitually. At least one person will be learning a new way to relate, where a sense of inner peace and certainty begins to expand and pent-up emotions and judgmental attitudes begin to release their grip.

The key with meditation is that it's not an isolated thing you do once or twice a day. As we're seeing here, what we learn when we take time to sit and meditate are mental tools we can also apply every active moment of each day. We don't become calmer, more patient, more honest, and more aware just during the time when we're meditating. The idea is to practice in meditation how we want to be every minute of the day.

Julie is already seeing this because several times during dinner she started to get really uptight with her parents or nervous with her boyfriend having dinner in her home. But as soon as she felt the tension starting to grip her breathing, rather than letting the whole negative reaction happen as it usually would, she did her best to stay aware of her breathing, to accept her feelings and breathe into them. By doing this, she found that she was able to relax a bit, just allow the moment happen, and do her best to enjoy herself. After all, it was great that her parents were being so nice to Danny, and even being open to a conversation about meditation.

The good news is that when something positive like that works a few times, we begin to do it more and more because we like the relief from our old reactions. That's how the experience of expanded awareness and relaxation that we discover in meditation can spread into our entire day—because it makes us feel better.

So much for talking about meditation, let's do it some more. After reading through the following meditation exercise, feel free to put the book aside, sit comfortably, close your eyes if you want, and just let yourself relax.

Begin to be aware of what's happening inside you, observe your inner feelings and thoughts without judging (we'll learn how to do that more specifically in the next chapter). Be sure to stay tuned into your breathing and to open up to the feelings in your heart.

Notice if you're choked up or breathing freely through your throat. Accept your inner feelings, and with each exhale allow the pressure inside you to begin to flow out. Go ahead and make sounds to help release your feelings, surrender to the feelings in your heart and let your breathing begin to heal whatever pains you might find there.

Remember to stay aware of the air flowing in and out of your nose or mouth, to feel the movement of your chest and belly as you breathe. Feel your heart, pounding right in the middle of your breathing. When you're ready, allow your thoughts and emotions to quiet down by focusing on two or more physical happenings or sensations in your body, your breathing and your heartbeat or the sounds around you, the sensations throughout your body. And as always, be open to a new experience.

pause and experience

CHAPTER 12

And Suddenly . . . Peace of Mind

Danny approached his house and noticed, as he got closer, that his breathing got tenser. He never knew if his dad was going to be in a good mood or ready to shout at him. He did have good times with his father sometimes, things weren't always terrible. But on weekends especially, when his dad started partying, Danny cringed—the alcohol and whatever else his dad might be consuming made him and his friends weird, not to mention sometimes aggressive.

But there was no one in the big old house when Danny let himself in with his key. All the lights were out; there wasn't a sound. The emptiness of the house made him think of his mom, and he wished she was here. Danny noticed immediately how, as he thought about his mom, his breathing got choked up, and a flush of anger mixed with tears tried to grab at him.

Trying to practice what he'd been learning from Julie and Lisa he did his best not to let his thoughts bum him out like they usually did. He could feel the solid weight of the meditation books in his hands, and remembered the new CD in his backpack. He flipped on some lights, went over to the living room, and put the CD on the stereo.

His dad would probably spend the night with his new girlfriend, since he wasn't back this late in the evening, so Danny had the house to himself. For just a moment the thought ran through his mind that maybe he would have Julie over sometime when his dad was gone, and that particular thought definitely changed how he felt in his body—in a totally good way.

The music came on. The soft jazz clarinet playing of Tony Scott and then the Japanese flute coming in as if in answer, and then the koto, too—he sat and just listened for a while, seeing if he could hold his attention on the music, and on his breathing, at the same time.

As his breathing settled his mind started thinking about Julie, and then about the Ping-Pong game with her father, and then Julie again, and her kiss. For a few moments, as he drifted into the past, and then into imaginings about how things might happen in the future, Danny lost awareness of his breathing and the music altogether, thinking about Julie and wondering what she was doing at that very moment.

Suddenly a creaky sound somewhere in the house jolted him and he tensed up, assuming his dad was coming home and the peace of the evening would be lost. But it had only been his cat coming in through the cat door in the kitchen. Sure enough, the old guy came trotting into the living room and right over into his lap.

Danny let his mind turn back to the music, and his breathing. He watched as four, five, six inhales and exhales came and went with him fully aware of the air flowing in and out, with his chest and belly naturally moving in and out with every breath. Each inhale seemed to have its own life, its own feeling, and each new one felt slightly different. He'd read at Julie's that a person never has the same experience twice, both in meditation and in all of life. And sure enough, as he watched his next inhale come and then turn into an exhale, he could see that it would be impossible to have two moments in life that were the same, because life was always new, always changing.

For a few more breaths Danny held his attention to the effortless comings and goings of his breathing. He let his breathing stop when it wanted to, and start again when it wanted to. Several times he sat quietly for ten, maybe twenty seconds without breathing at all, immersed in total stillness, relaxation, and calm . . . then the next breath would come on its own.

The thought went through his mind that, right then, everything was okay in his life. His dad was gone and not a bother; he was doing well in school and on the Ping-Pong team, and most important, he had Julie in his life—someone who loved him just as he was.

As he realized that everything was okay in his life, he began to experience in his chest, and then in his whole body, the strangest sensation. It was as if his awareness was expanding and filling not only his whole body but the whole room. Without any effort, the air came flowing into him, and then on its own flowed out of him again, and the music flowed on and on. Just then the most exquisite feeling of bliss came rushing through his entire being—nothing changed, breaths came and went, the music kept flowing. All that was different was that his thoughts were entirely quiet, his emotions pure, calm, and bright. His heart felt remarkably expansive and his awareness seemed to be everywhere at once, uniting him with everything around him.

Then the CD clicked off. The experience, which had been so expansive, dropped back to more normal realms, but the good calm peaceful feeling inside him continued. He realized he was sleepy, and utterly content, and headed up to his bed.

~~~~~~~~~~~~~~

As we just saw, the benefits of meditation are often subtle, and can't be manipulated into happening. Inner peace isn't something we work actively to get close to and then manage to grab hold of. Peace of mind comes only when we quietly allow it to come, like a bird or other wild animal will come to us sometimes if we just relax.

That's what happened with Danny unexpectedly that evening. He had learned only a small bit about meditation so far, but by simply pausing and opening up to the basic process of watching his breaths come and go, and watching his thoughts come and go, he temporarily let go of his mind's grip on life. And as if by magic, he expanded into a deep experience of spiritual awareness.

There's a lot of talk about what it means to be spiritual. As we're using the term here, being spiritual is actually a very simple notion. When we choose to open our hearts and accept whatever each new moment offers us, when we calm down and tune into our honest feelings, when we let go of our grip on life and surrender to what "is," then we are allowing our consciousness to expand and we come more into harmony with the depths of life. This is what we mean when we talk about having a spiritual experience.

When our hearts are touched, when our emotions become clear and calm, when we stop trying to make things happen and instead just allow them to happen—this is when we enter into a universal state of awareness where we can experience the truth of each new moment. This is when we can discover our spiritual depths—right in the middle of that moment. In a nutshell, that's meditation.

Let's end this second part with the basic meditation process we've been exploring bit by bit so far in this book. Remember that, especially with meditation, true learning isn't a sudden onetime experience. We learn by moving through the same basic inner process over and over, and each and every time, going deeper. The spiritual truth is that your inner reality is infinite and, at the same time, readily accessible—as long as you remember to look within regularly and to stay open to new experiences.

These guided experiences will teach you specific mental habits that, after a while, will come automatically, so that you become entirely your own guide.

In part one we learned the "Breath Meditation," which is the first step in this general meditation program—where you turn your focus of attention fully to the experience of your breathing sensations in your nose and in your chest and belly. This primal meditation process tunes you deeply into your own presence, alive in this eternally unfolding present moment. This "here and now" experience is the foundation of all successful meditation.

Once you've brought yourself "here and now" you're ready to expand your awareness with another crucial step that is also universal in all meditation traditions: becoming more aware of your heart right in the middle of your breathing. The meditation path is without question a heart path, and regularly focusing your loving attention to your own heart is vital to waking up spiritually.

Of course, when you first tune into your heart feelings, as we found with Danny and Lisa and Julie, you're liable to encounter emotions that are upsetting, that outright hurt inside your chest. What we also saw was that the process of turning your attention to your hurt or angry feelings activates a healing and release process that will free you from your inner suffering—this is another primary reason to meditate!

We often hope we have friends who will love us just as we are and help us heal our upset feelings through their love, but the truth is that unless we first learn to accept and love our own selves, other people just can't help us. This is why meditation on a daily basis can be such a radical, positive thing to do: Meditation is the purposeful act of regularly turning our loving attention inward to our heart so that something good and healing can happen inside our own selves.

So, as you turn your mind's attention in this second meditation to your own heart and whatever you find there, trust that each time you do this, and breathe into what you find without judgment, you'll be activating a healing process that will help you let go of bad feelings and open yourself to good feelings.

Meditation is all about love. And love is the only thing that heals heartaches and upset feelings. And where does that love come from?

Throughout this book we'll be exploring the meditative answer to that giant question. All great spiritual teachers have taught that God is love, and that when we open our hearts to God, we're opening ourselves to receive love. It's that infinite love that permeates the universe, that comes rushing into our hearts when we pause, turn inward, accept what we find in our hearts, and open up to the healing love that meditation brings into our hearts.

This process is so important to a good life, and yet how often do we pause and open our hearts? A daily meditation practice is designed to make sure that you nurture your heart regularly so that the painful feelings you accumulate can receive loving attention and be healed. So breathe into your inner feelings, let love flow in, and as you release your pent-up feelings, you can relax and deeply enjoy this second phase of our meditation program!

By the time you come to the end of this book you'll have learned a full meditation program that you can move through in a couple of minutes when you're in action, or take ten to thirty minutes to enjoy when you're able to relax and settle into meditation. You're already learning to master the first meditative expansion, the "Breath Meditation." Now we're going to move through that first step and then go right on into the second step of our process, "Heart Awakening."

MEDITATION TWO
Heart Awakening
(Letting the Emotions Flow)

To begin, let yourself move a bit, stretch if you want to, get entirely comfortable. Temporarily let go of all your thoughts about the past and the future and give yourself full permission to relax into this present moment.

Take the time to notice how your breaths are naturally coming and going, tune into the sensation of the air flowing in and out through your nose or mouth with every new breath. Now expand your awareness to also experience the rhythmic movements in your chest and belly as you breathe.

Make no effort to inhale or exhale, let your breathing stop when it wants to and start when it wants to. After your breathing stops, notice the spark of life deep within you, which again brings the air rushing in and out, through your nose or mouth; go ahead and set your breathing free.

Now, as you stay aware of the breathing sensations in your nose and chest and belly, expand your awareness to include the feelings in your heart, right in the middle of your breathing.

Begin to notice if your heart feels good, or if there's any tension, pain, or pressure within your chest. Accept what you find, be your own best friend and be loving toward yourself. Say to yourself: "I accept myself just as I am."

And now also tune into the feelings in your throat; notice if you're at all choked up. Let your tongue relax, and your jaw muscles, breathe through your mouth if you feel under pressure inside, make any sounds that express what you are feeling. And with each new exhale, let the pressure and those feelings come rushing out. Release whatever feelings you find inside you, set them free, love them, and let them heal.

If this feels good to you, then you can choose to open your heart; if it hurts, know that a closed heart always aches. An open heart is able to heal and love again, so choose to open your heart. Say to yourself: "My heart is open to receive."

And with each new breath, whatever your personal sense of God, go ahead and inhale God's healing love into your heart. Choose to allow your heart to expand, to heal, as you begin to feel better and better inside your own heart.

Breathe and let the feelings in your body change as you tune into whatever emotions might be under pressure inside you, wanting some friendly loving attention.

When you're ready, completely calm yourself down inside. As your breathing lets go of emotions and settles into a more relaxed rhythm, you release just enough of your feelings to make you feel a bit lighter, more satisfied inside your own skin, and free from some of the pressure of life.

Allow your breathing to flow more smoothly with each new inhale and exhale. And choose for the next moments to tune into purely enjoyable feelings inside you. Let your breathing relax, your heart soften. Right now everything is okay; you can fully enjoy this moment of your life. You're free inside your heart to take a breather and just enjoy the sensation of your next breaths. Let your breathing come effortlessly as you focus within and open to a new experience.

pause and experience

Part Three
MIND AWARENESS
(Learning the Seven Focus Phrases)

Now that we've begun to understand how our breathing and our emotions are intimately related, it's time to focus specifically on the third dimension of consciousness that determines how we feel and what we do in life: the thoughts, beliefs, and mental habits that stimulate our emotions.

Meditation is all about learning how to watch (without judgment) all the thoughts that habitually run through your mind—and then to quiet those thoughts so that your emotions become calm and life becomes better all around.

This section is really the heart of the program, because in these chapters you'll learn the seven focus phrases that will make meditation easy to master. By simply memorizing these seven sentences, and then remembering them whenever you want to meditate, whether for one minute or one hour, you'll have the perfect inner guidance for moving through the full seven meditative expansions.

This section is also the heart of the program because it brings together everything we've been learning and unifies our hearts and our minds into a greater, more expansive experience of life. Each of the seven meditative expansions of consciousness presented in this section will lead you deeper into your own heart as you discover the remarkable power of love as it flows through your personal life.

This part focuses on the interaction between our seemingly constant flow of internal thoughts and our newly emerging meditative experience. In the first two sections you began to explore how to tune into the present moment through breath awareness, expanding into heart awareness. Now we're specifically focusing on the third step, that of observing your thoughts in action, learning to step back from your thoughts rather than identify them, and how to quiet that flow altogether whenever you want to—freedom!

We're going to explore how our thinking minds all too often carry negative expectancies, and how that creates worries about something bad happening in our lives. And these thoughts and negative imaginations about the future very often inhibit what we might do in life, and keep us from opening up to something good.

We've seen in the first two meditations, breath and heart, how vital it is to quiet our worried minds and shift into a present-moment experiencing of life. The basic psychological fact is that we can't be lost in thought, which is mostly about the past or the future, and at the same time be fully engaged in experiencing the present moment. Meditation teaches us how to shift away from our chronic thoughts into the infinite potential of the present moment. But often we find that we just can't break free from our thoughts—they keep filling our minds with all their worries and problem-solving busyness.

A lot of people feel they're total victims of their thought flows, to the point where there's almost never any peace of mind or calm good feelings in the heart. Here we will explore how meditation can help us stop worrying and stop judging everything around us so that we can regularly enjoy the pleasure and insights that come to us when our thoughts are quiet and our experience of the present moment is our central focus.

CHAPTER 13

Thoughts and Emotions

The phone rang in Danny's living room and his father, who was sitting watching a ball game on television, took it.

"George here, what's up?" he said in his usual casual voice.

"Hi George, this is Peter, your boy Dan has been over at our house quite a lot; he's good friends with our daughter, Julie."

"Oh, well, what kind of trouble is he in, what's he done?"

"Nothing like that, he's a perfect gentleman; we enjoy his company."

"Oh," George said.

"We were just wondering if you and Dan would like to come over for a barbecue this weekend, Saturday afternoon around four. We're having a few friends over and would like to meet you, too. What do you say?"

George sat there a moment, half his concentration still on the ball game. He was ready to say no, he wasn't much in the mood to socialize with strangers. But then he had a twinge of guilt at not being much involved with his boy's life. "Uh, I'm not sure what I'm doing this weekend," he said. "But thanks for asking. I'll have Danny get back to you."

He hung up and went back to watching the ball game.

Danny came into the house a while later, said hi and headed toward the stairs.

"Hey, wait a minute," George said. "Some guy named Peter phoned and out of the blue invited us to some barbecue. Said you're hanging out with his daughter a lot. What's this, you have a girlfriend and don't even tell me?"

Danny took a deep breath, expecting anything, but his dad was in a good mood, and just grinned. "Well, I'm glad you're getting out there finally with the girls," George said. "What's her name? Oh, he said it: Julie?"

"Uh, yep."

"So what do you say, shall we go grab some free grub? Are these people I'll get along with, or some uptight religious types? Barbecue with no beer doesn't grab me."

"Oh, they're real nice people, not uptight at all. And they drink wine with dinner, so I'm sure there'll be some beer. Why? You'd want to go? Really?"

"Lucy is gone this weekend, nothing much to do. And I've got to check out this girl you're hanging with, don't I? Why haven't you brought her around the house?"

Danny noticed his breathing was not happening at all. He was ready to just duck out of the conversation with his dad, but then he caught himself and chose to stand there and be honest. "Well, to be honest, I haven't brought her around because I never know what might be happening here."

George took in what his boy had said. His expression clouded and he almost shouted something in reaction. But instead he cocked his head, thought a moment, and turned off the sound of the ball game.

"What? You're ashamed of your home?"

"Dad, you know that when you're drinking you upset me, you shout at me. You'd scare Julie. That's just the reality of it. What do you expect me to do?"

Again, George was ready to react, but he was a bit jolted by his boy standing there like a man, saying his truth. "Hmm," he said, remembering how Lucy had the habit of running around in the buff, and imagining that maybe Danny had a point. "Well, whatever," he said. "Just tell me, do you want me to make this effort and go to some barbecue and all?"

Danny felt twinges of apprehension at the thought of his dad maybe making a fool of himself at the barbecue. But on the other hand . . . "I'd like it, Dad," he said. "They're good people, I like them, and Julie's just, well, do you really want to go?"

"Hey, free grub, why not? You tell them, okay?"

Slightly shocked by his dad's willingness to go, Danny said okay and headed up the stairs two at a time, not sure if he was eager or apprehensive. He closed his door, sat down on his bed, his head buzzing with scenarios of what might happen with his dad at the barbecue. Remembering to watch his breathing and tune into his heart, he found a giant ache. When he looked to see what thoughts were running through his head, he found a bunch: his dad getting drunk and bothersome at the barbecue; the fact that he didn't have a mother at home who would go, too; the painful memories of times when all three had gone to neighborhood events together. And that led to thoughts about how there was something wrong with his parents and, worse, with him that had made his family fall apart.

Stimulated by these negative thoughts, he felt a terrible ache in his heart and realized how much he missed his parents not being together anymore. But as he bravely kept focused right within his heart and all those bad feelings, like Lisa had encouraged, he remembered to relax his jaw and let the feelings come flowing out, and doing that, the pressure inside him started to ease up.

Again negative thoughts tried to pull him down, but then he remembered that, recently, his dad had not been acting so weird, that things had been better around the house, and that he was surviving without his mom at home. Now that he had Julie in his life, everything was improving. He even found that he was able to imagine his father actually enjoying talking with Peter, they were similar in a lot of ways—and there was hope that the afternoon could turn out okay.

With that shift in thought, Danny found all his emotions shifting for the better. The barbeque would be a risk, but he was willing to take the risk in hopes that something good might come from it. And with that thought in mind, he again turned his focus to his breathing . . . and found that with Julie in his heart, he could relax and settle into just being in the present moment.

~~~~~~~~~~~~~~~~~~

Danny's case is a bit extreme for most home situations, but we all must face the risk of something bad happening in the hope of something good happening. The first step in all of this is simply the realization that our thoughts are what generate our emotional suffering. Danny, for instance, is beginning to realize that each time he gets hit with the agony of missing his mother, there's a thought that stimulates the agony: a thought that tells him he needs his mother to survive, a thought that tells him his life is impossible without his mother, a thought that tells him he's somehow no good, that he's been rejected, that his mother doesn't love him and therefore no one can love him.

These are the thoughts he sees coming to mind regularly, often just barely on the surface of his consciousness, that immediately stimulate the aching in his heart. And he's finding in meditation that he can catch these negative assumptions, see that they're dominating his mind, and question whether they're true or not. Our core beliefs and assumptions about life are developed when we are young, and all too often they're just plain wrong or based on a situation that no longer prevails. Meditation helps us look honestly at our inner assumptions and reactions and see clearly if they're still valid or if they should be put aside.

Danny can feel the pain in his heart where his mother once was. But when he meditates and moves through that pain, he also finds the love he feels for Julie. He can look and see clearly that he can survive without his mother in the house, that he can find other people to love him, and that he can feel good in his heart because he's choosing to feel good—he's free!

He's also discovering in meditation that he can accept reality, and that this step of accepting things just as they are rather than fighting them is a powerfully liberating inner act of the mind. He is learning step by step that when he accepts that what his mother did was simply what she had to do, then he can forgive her, and in that act of forgiving her, he is discovering a new sense of being connected with her, and that feels wonderful, too.

He's also looking at his father in this new light, and seeing what's really true rather than what he's expecting based on past experiences. For instance, he paused on the stairs and decided to talk with his father about the barbecue because in his last meditation, he'd seen that he was afraid of his father in general, and expected his father to always do things that were embarrassing or frightening. But as he looked over the last few months, he saw that his father was calming down and being more considerate. Something was happening inside his father that was changing things, and when Danny gave his father half a chance, it seemed that good feelings were happening more and more. Danny finally realized that his dad must have been shattered when his wife left him, and maybe he'd been on his binge because of that.

You might want to pause right now, put the book aside, and reflect on any negative assumptions you may have about your parents, friends, or yourself. Just pause a bit, watch your breathing, tune into your heart, bring one of these negative thoughts to mind, see how you feel about this person or thing, and be open to new insights and feelings about them or it.

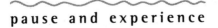

pause and experience

CHAPTER 14

How Our Minds Really Work

~~~~~~~~~~~~~~~~~~~~~~

Friday afternoon, Lisa's dad, Robert, had offered to help her with a school paper she was trying to write as a team project for science, about cognitive psychology and the study of how thoughts relate to emotions. Her partner was a boy named Kent who Lisa was starting to like, and in more ways than just scholarly. He walked home with her after school, and they had a snack in the kitchen. Lisa's mom was shopping so they had the house to themselves until Robert got home from work, or until Julie and Dan came by.

Kent was tall and quiet, not at all a jock like Lisa's last boyfriend. Kent was smart and sometimes funny and had deep brown eyes that Lisa loved to look into because she didn't feel they were judging her, just watching in a very kind, interested way. She took him up to the meditation room. She'd already told him that she was interested in the assignment because she liked to meditate, and meditation was all about how our thoughts influence us and how we can get beyond them when we want to go deeper. Kent had listened to all this and just nodded. He didn't seem to have any goofy ideas about meditation, and they'd already done some reading together at school, about studies showing how different kinds of thoughts stimulate different emotional reactions in the body. They'd also studied cognitive psychology books that talked about how changing the way you think about things directly changes the emotions you feel, and how this is used in therapy to help depressed people stop thinking negative thoughts and start thinking brighter thoughts that improve feelings.

Lisa settled down on one pillow and Kent sat across from her on another. For a moment they were quiet. Lisa felt nervous, being alone with a new boy whom she liked so much. She tried to calm herself with her breathing, but when she looked to her heart she found it so excited that she just had to laugh.

"What's so funny?" he asked her curiously.

"Oh, just that I've been meditating for two years now and should be a pro at calming myself down, but I'm not."

They eyed each other and smiled, both a bit bashful.

"This is a cool room," he said.

"Yeah, it's my favorite, I come in here at least once a day, just to sit and quiet down and look to see what's up inside."

"I was trying to do what you were talking about yesterday," he said, "to just watch my thoughts go by without getting involved with them. That's hard. My mind is always in gear."

"Mine, too, but there are some neat tricks," she said. "Maybe my dad will talk about them a little, he's the family expert about psychology, he reads all sorts of books on the mind."

"Well, can you show me how to do it? How does somebody learn meditation?"

Lisa smiled at that.

"Something funny about that?" he asked, but not defensively, just wondering why that beautiful smile came across her lips.

"It's just that people keep asking that question," she explained. "Every day recently, a couple of friends and I have been sitting here with me doing my best to teach them the basics of how to meditate. You know, you can join us if you want, sometime."

"What's it cost a session?"

She laughed again. "An apple," she joked. "Want to try the very first step with me?"

Kent and Lisa both had their eyes closed and were practicing the primary two-step breath awareness technique, which she had just explained to him, when a knock came on the door to the meditation room and their eyes popped open.

Robert had arrived home from work and came walking into the room. Kent stood up and the two men shook hands. Lisa watched her father's expression carefully and was relieved to see that he didn't seem to be doing any judging. They chatted a while about school and the writing project, and then Robert made himself comfortable with them.

"I'm not an expert," he said and made sure Kent understood. "It's just a hobby of mine, trying to figure out how the minds works. If I was your age, I think that's what I'd want to study and spend my whole life caught up in; it's definitely the next frontier—and I'm glad to see the two of you already so eager to take a look for yourselves."

The front door buzzed and Lisa jumped up to run down and see who it was, hoping it was Julie and Dan. And sure enough, there the two of them stood, holding hands, looking almost overly happy together.

And so the four high schoolers and Robert found themselves sitting together, as Robert did his best to explain the basics of how the thinking mind works according to cognitive psychology, which he said was by far the most successful therapy technique developed so far.

In the late sixties, a professor named Aaron Beck at the University of Pennsylvania first developed the formal psychological understanding of how our habitual thought-flows in turn stimulate emotions and mood. He also demonstrated how we can choose to take control of our minds and think more positive, realistic thoughts—thoughts that directly encourage a positive boost in mood. From this basic realization emerged the entire cognitive therapy movement that now dominates the therapy world.

"If you need some quotes on all that, or just want to read more, I have a number of texts downstairs you can borrow," Robert offered. "There are also several new meditation books that teach how to integrate Buddhist breath meditation into a therapy program. This is a hopeful period of history we're lucky enough to be living in, where the deeper spiritual healing techniques are beginning to be integrated into psychology."

"My mom was in a kind of cognitive therapy for a while," Kent put in, "but it didn't seem to do her much good. She found out she was carrying around a lot of negative beliefs about herself that were causing her to get depressed a lot. Just seeing that helped her—and me, too. During her therapy period she went around the house talking to herself all the time, putting positive thoughts into her mind. But somehow that didn't entirely do the trick—I don't think she got along with her therapist very well—and she went back on medication, which leaves her slightly lost somehow. A lot of the time, now, she doesn't take any pills at all, she says she'd rather suffer through the depressive times than be a zombie. I think she's getting better, and what I'm wondering is, would meditation help her?"

"It's very possible," Robert answered. "And the reason is this: Cognitive therapy helps people change from having negative thoughts and attitudes, to positive thoughts and attitudes. It often works, up to a point. But for all its pluses, what is it lacking?" He looked to Lisa for the answer, not wanting to just sit and spout all his theories while everyone else sat and listened.

"Oh, that's easy," she said. "I mean, I've heard you talking about this before. In cognitive therapy, there's still no training in how to quiet the mind altogether. And like you and Mom are always saying, there's no real healing taking place until the ego shuts up and lets the higher self go to into action, and that's what meditation does."

"Well, all that's easy to say," Danny put in, "but most of the time I find it really hard to make my mind shut up. More often than not, it just keeps on talking nonstop."

"We all have that challenge," Robert agreed. "And if you want, maybe we should explore some of the new psychological insights into how to quiet the mind and the ancient meditative techniques as well, if you're interested. It should fit into the theme of your paper."

"Please," Kent said. "That's what I'm here for."

"Okay then, let's start with the most basic discovery in perceptual psychology: When you focus your mind on two or more sensory happenings at the same time—like your breathing and your heartbeat, or your foot and your head, or a sound and a sight—all thought immediately stops."

"If it's that simple," Dan put in, "then why doesn't everyone get taught that in school?"

"Maybe the teachers haven't yet learned the value of a quiet mind themselves," Robert offered.

"When you tune into the sensations of the air flowing in and out of your nose," Julie said, "and at the same time tune into the movements in your chest and belly as you breathe—there you have it. Two sensations at once: quiet mind."

"And the ancient spiritual teachers," Robert pointed out, "knew this psychological fact long ago, just from their own experience. Almost every ancient meditation technique the world over uses this basic breath awareness to quiet thoughts. That's what Buddha's Vipassana meditation is all about, for instance. From what I hear, Lisa is already doing a great job explaining to Dan and Julie the beginning process."

"She's a good teacher," Julie said.

"Well, it works for me for maybe a few minutes," Danny put in, "but then I get lost in thinking again. When I'm here in this room meditating with other people, it seems pretty easy. I get quiet and relaxed and go through my feelings, and sometimes into this amazing place inside me, where it's . . . I can't really explain it, except that I like it. But then when I go home and try to meditate alone, usually I get impatient after a few minutes and don't go any further."

"Well," Robert offered, "you're probably ready to learn about focus phrases."

"Focus phrases?"

"In most meditative traditions, certain sayings or chants, mantras, are used to help focus attention deeper inside and to quiet thoughts. Psychologists have recently found just how effective such focus phrases can be in helping us to remember an entire inner mental process. If you want to, we can talk about the basic focus phrases that seem to work best in meditation, for pointing your attention in worthwhile directions. It's amazing how easy they can make meditation, and how effective they are in moving you deeper and deeper into whatever new experience is coming to you each time you pause to look inside."

"Wait—you mean you use words to quiet words?" Julie asked, not quite understanding.

"Exactly, you give your thinking mind something worthwhile to do, remembering and holding in your mind these special phrases. In that way you keep the ego busy and make it a valuable participant in meditation, so it doesn't feel left out. You'd be surprised how well this works."

"Okay, what are the focus phrases?" Kent asked.

"The phrases won't surprise you," Robert went on, "because they're drawn from the actual meditation process, following how the mind expands step by step. Probably Lisa has been saying the first ones already to you. First of all, when you sit down to meditate, after getting comfortable, you can immediately aim your attention exactly where you want it by saying to yourself: 'I feel the air, flowing in and out, through my nose.' Or, if your nose is stuffed that day, say 'mouth.'

"Try it yourselves right now, don't take my word for it. Say: 'I feel the air, flowing in and out, through my nose.' Say it a few *times. Allow the words to point your attention in that exact sensory direction.*

"Once you're fully tuned into the sensation in your nose," Robert *went on, "go ahead and say the second focus phrase. This will expand your awareness so that it's focused on two sensations at once: 'I feel the movements in my chest and belly as I breathe.'*

As we go deeper into meditation, you'll find this verbal-cue process of using the focus phrases Robert is teaching to be invaluable in your progress. Rather than your mind trying to remember everything you're supposed to do in the meditation flow, all you need to do is memorize the short focus phrases, and each time you pause to meditate, these verbal cues will guide you through the ever-deepening experience of looking within.

We'll be learning seven focus phrases in all, and these key statements will be all you need, after a couple weeks of practice, to master this meditation program. So rather than thinking you're going to have to memorize everything in this book, you can just relax, enjoy the read, and rest assured that by the time you've finished reading the book, you'll know by heart the seven focus phrases that point you inward. You'll know how to open up to the infinity of experience that lies directly within and beyond.

For now, let's settle a bit deeper into the first two focus phrases. They're very simple and straightforward. You don't have to ruminate upon them; you simply do what you're telling yourself to do. You take positive charge of your mind and aim your all-powerful focus of attention right to the heart of your true being.

You already know the first two focus phrases by heart because they summarize what Lisa has been teaching her friends thus far. What's new and powerful is the actual act of saying them to yourself. You're learning by heart the superstructure of meditation, the formula for success. As Robert pointed out, you're giving the part of yourself that usually interrupts your meditations something helpful to do during meditation, and this activity will mostly satisfy and occupy the chatter center of your brain.

Our thinking minds are genetically programmed to protect us by anticipating bad things that might happen in the future and making plans and actions that will enable us to avoid those bad things. This is all fine and good when kept in its place. The human dilemma is that this fear-based function of the mind seems to have taken over, and meditation is the process whereby we calmly insist on spending only a certain amount of our day thinking and problem solving. All the rest of the day we can spend enjoying ourselves and awakening our deeper potential, here in this eternal present moment.

Okay, go ahead and give these two elicitor phrases a try so you can experience for yourself the power of these special "self-guiding" statements to instantly and effortlessly point you directly where you want to focus. Read the two focus phrases below a couple of times so that you pretty much know them by heart. Then feel free to close your eyes and say the first statement, and experience the "nose" sensation for a few breaths. Then say the second, "chest," statement, and expand to include that new experience along with the "nose" sensation—in a word, allow your mind's focus to turn in the direction you yourself are suggesting:

"I feel the air, flowing in and out, through my nose."

"I feel the movements in my chest and belly, as I breathe."

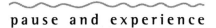

pause and experience

CHAPTER 15
Heart and Mind Together

Robert opened his eyes and watched the four teenagers quietly sitting in the room with him, their eyes closed as they focused intently on their breathing experience and whatever might open up to them through this inner focusing. He thought back to his own childhood of forced religious attendance, and realized just how happy he was that the new generation was getting to choose for themselves how they wanted to approach their spiritual exploration and identity.

Ten minutes or so later, everyone had their eyes open again, and Robert was ready to teach them the next logical step in meditation, and therefore the next logical focus phrase.

"Who can guess what the next focus might be?" he asked.

"Well, it's bound to be the heart," Danny said. "Actually Lisa already told us. And for me that's sometimes easy and sometimes almost impossible."

"You're not alone there," Robert assured him. "You'd be surprised how hard it is for the average person to turn their focus to their heart. I recently read an interview by one of the founders of a research group called 'Heart-Math,' talking about a study they did that showed how most of the people in the study usually found it upsetting or scary to turn their mind's attention to their own heart. Why do you suppose that's is? The heart, after all, is supposed to be the beautiful center of love in our lives."

"I know why," Danny said, "at least for me. I've got all kinds of emotions inside me down there, and a lot of them are ones I don't really want to focus on because they hurt. But now that Lisa has helped me see that I end up feeling better after tuning into my

heart even when it hurts, I'm starting to see that it's worth doing. But still, every time I get to that third step of being aware of my heart, it's scary. Sometimes I can't even remember what the third step is, so I'll guess that the focus phrase is something like what Lisa says over and over: 'I'm aware of my heart, right in the middle of my breathing.' "

Robert smiled at Lisa, then said to the group, "That's it exactly. And again, there's nothing complex or difficult, just the specific words pointing toward the desired experience. I suppose Lisa has talked a bit about how to move through hurt feelings and fear and all the rest, when you look to your heart and find them there?"

"Yep," said Danny. "And I've got to say, mostly it works. In fact, that's what I like best about meditation so far. It helps me blow off steam rather than blowing my stack like I used to do all the time. Not that I don't still blow up now and then, but already it's getting better."

"Ah, that's wonderful to hear, Dan. Okay, any questions before we put all three of these focus phrases together?"

"One thing," Julie said. "Am I supposed to actually feel my heart beating inside me, or what? Sometimes I can't find my heartbeat at all, but I sure find the emotions. And sometimes I'm just numb inside."

Robert was quiet a moment, reflecting. "Well, there are no set rules about how to tune into the heart, we just have to point our attention there and experience what we find that moment. Being aware of our hearts is something gigantic," he said finally, "and the experience just expands on and on all our lives if we let it. Our heart in so many ultimate ways is our very core of being. It feels everything, it's the seat of true wisdom, it tunes us into God's healing touch, and it's the epicenter of our experiencing selves. Listen to me, I even turn into a poet when I talk about it. Anyway, I don't want to give any set rules or expectations about what experience to look for or what to expect when you make this third giant step inside your own universe. The focus phrase will effortlessly turn your attention in that direction and allow you to discover for yourself what's happening in your heart at that moment. And that's what meditation is all about: discovery."

"Well, maybe I don't want to find out what's there," Kent said soberly. "Maybe I'll do better not getting caught up in all that heart mess."

"That's definitely what a lot of people feel," Robert concurred. "They want to avoid tapping into the feelings in their heart because some of them hurt, and hurt bad. But look at it this way: If your heart is the center of your entire life experience, either you accept the painful feelings you find there and let them heal, or you become numb and go around hardly alive at all. When you look at the choice, and also remember that the heart does heal, and that love does come flowing into your heart when you allow it, well, the choice is yours. You know the saying, you can lead a horse to water but you can't make him drink. Meditation, and these focus phrases in particular, lead your attention to the water, but you must choose to open up. I don't mean to be harsh. I just want to say that each moment, each of us is choosing to have our hearts open or closed. And meditation offers a safe, healing path for opening the heart."

Robert paused and looked into the eyes of each of the four people with him, one after the other. He could see the brightness, the eagerness, the pioneer spirit in each of them, he felt he could feel deeply, right then, each of their vulnerable hearts, and he felt momentarily elated and wordless.

"The bottom line for me is this," he said, softly. "Spirit touches us and God's love comes flowing into us only when we're open and aware in our hearts. As we move through these steps in meditation, we're moving toward opening our hearts to the greater reality, and receiving insights and healing and just plain old wonderful loving feelings. Let's try it now with all three of the *focus phrases, one after the other, taking a few breaths with each, so you really experience that step before expanding to include the next step . . . just close your eyes, and say to yourself:*

"I feel the air, flowing in and out, through my nose."

"I feel the movements in my chest and belly as I breathe."

"I'm aware of my heart right in the middle of my breathing."

~~~~~~~~~~~~~~~~

This primary focus on the heart's role in meditation can never be overemphasized, because in all traditions, meditation is by definition "the heart path," and learning to hold our focus on the heart is absolutely key to walking that path. The heart is the spiritual gateway to infinite realization and the experience of who we really are beyond our thinking mind's confining beliefs and assumptions.

Even imbedded in our language, we recognize that the heart is more than a blood pump. Take the saying "speaking from the heart," for example. Recent neurological studies show that when we are busy thinking in our mighty forebrains, a major nerve sends messages down to the heart related to what we're thinking, and then the heart sends messages in response back to that thinking part of the brain, resulting in actual conscious thought. This potent neurological connection between heart and brain indicates that our thinking not only stimulates feelings in the heart but that the response of the heart also influences the flow of our thoughts.

Even more startling research has documented that the actual tissue material that makes up the heart isn't just regular muscle tissue. Actually, upwards of 60 percent of the tissue of the heart is almost identical to the neurological cells of the brain. This discovery has led researchers to talk about the heart as "the fifth brain" of the body, mysteriously and intimately hooked up with the four main brain centers in the skull that we talked about earlier.

Thus our language enables us to talk about "the wisdom of the heart" when we're being sincere and expressing our most honest feelings in conversation. The medical research just cited shows that this saying isn't just a metaphor; we actually do have the neurological ability to speak from the heart. The scientific study of all this is just beginning to take off, and promises radical insights into who we really are and what we might aspire to, especially in terms of using meditation to activate our hearts more fully into our usual mental activity and communications.

In your own experience, you'll want to approach this third expansion of consciousness in meditation slowly. If you're like most people, you're going to find a lot of emotions stuffed down out of sight in your heart that beg attention and healing. What's important is to give yourself time, and don't judge all your feelings as good or bad. As we're discovering, your own acceptance and love of your buried emotions will heal the "bad" painful contractions in your heart, so that your heart can sing again.

What's important here is developing the meditative habit to regularly pause, if only for one minute, to move through the focus phrases and inner expansions of awareness that bring you into direct experiential contact with your own heart and the feelings therein. Not only does practice make perfect in this inner act, but every time you move through the process of looking to your heart and feeling honestly what's there, you generate positive change and healing in your emotions. Instead of remaining a victim of your inner anguish, you take charge and do something about it.

It's quite amazing (or downright depressing, depending on how you look at it) that we live in a society that can send people to the moon but doesn't teach each new generation basic meditational tools that will enable them to know their own hearts and heal whatever emotional aches are found there. This book is dedicated to taking us beyond the "ignorance is bliss" attitude about emotions so that more and more people can begin to live and act more from their hearts. All the great spiritual teachers have agreed that this is the only path that will lead to world peace and equality, fairness, and, ultimately, wonderful times for everyone. And each of us has the responsibility to learn to open up more to love so we can, in turn, share that love wherever we go.

Let us move once again through the process we're trying to master so that your heart, as well as your head, learns the process. As you say each of the focus phrases in turn, take time to open up and experience the unique new moment that you discover within. And as you tune into your breathing, and then your heart, see what happens when you accept whatever you find, breathe into your emotional pressures, and let the pressures flow out and be gone.

And remember, you can do this heart meditation anytime, anywhere, so that almost continually, you help your heart wake up, heal its pains, and come alive with love in each new emerging moment:

"I feel the air, flowing in and out, through my nose."

"I feel the movements in my chest and belly as I breathe."

"I'm aware of my heart right in the middle of my breathing."

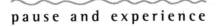

pause and experience

CHAPTER 16
Meditative Focus Phrases

Again everyone in the room spent about ten minutes doing the meditation together, this time employing the three focus phrases. And again Robert opened his eyes a little early and watched the four young adults in the room as they looked inward to their own hearts and emotions. Lisa and Danny were breathing through their mouths when Robert first looked, while emotions calmed down inside them.

At a certain point everyone but Kent had their eyes open, and they were all watching Kent, who seemed to have gone deeply into some very calm peaceful place. When his eyes opened, he looked almost guilty as he met their grins.

"Well," he said, "it got so relaxed I could have stayed there forever, just watching my breaths coming and going. Really— amazing."

Robert smiled. "Looks like we have a natural here. Good going. Anyway, have we covered enough ground for today?"

"What's the next focus phrase, I'm curious," Danny asked.

"Well, there are a couple of variations on the next theme," Robert explained. "And of course nothing here is written in cement, I'm just teaching you what works best for me. You may want to modify your own program. But the next step as I like it, once we've tuned into the present moment with the breathing, and then expanded to the heart and let whatever emotions we find have a chance to settle down, is to go right through the 'quiet mind' step. First, why would you want to quiet your mind anyway?"

Everyone was quiet a moment. Lisa knew the answer, or at least her answer, but on purpose she didn't speak up. And Julie stepped right in. "Your wife was telling us about the different parts of the brain," she remembered, "and how the conceptual part tends to dominate us because it's the part that looks out for danger and solves our problems and makes plans and so forth. The logical part, I think she said. And as long as that talk-talk part of the mind is in gear, all the other parts of the mind don't get a chance to contribute."

"I couldn't have said that better myself," Robert said.

"I have a different sense of it," Danny put in. "Already, I get the point that most of the time, when I'm thinking, I'm worrying about the future. Either that or I'm back in the past remembering something that happened that upset me, and mulling over it— especially running all these arguments with my dad through my head, what I would say to him to defend my side of an argument. And it's like Lisa says—we make ourselves suffer because of all the thoughts that just keep gushing through our minds. That's what I want to stop—those thoughts that keep me stirred up emotionally and not able to just enjoy life."

Robert nodded. "Okay, there are two main things you can do, Dan, and of course the rest of you, too, because we all get caught in thoughts that drag us down. The first step is to do nothing except just observe our recurrent thoughts and themes so that we see clearly what we're doing to ourselves. Buddha taught that process in his Vipassana meditation, Krishnamurti taught the same lesson—that if we want to change a negative habit, all we have to do is watch it in action and see that it makes us suffer. And that seeing, in itself, will generate change for the better. That seems to be one of the most important facts of meditation: To see a negative habit clearly is to evoke positive growth inside."

"Okay, I think I agree with you," Dan said. "But what do I do when my thoughts just consume me so much that I lose any awareness of my breathing altogether? I keep going off on these mental tangents, worrying about something, remembering

something, that leaves me entirely spaced out—and usually feeling awful."

"Okay, again, that's universal," Robert said, "and meditation does offer the solution. Remember the basic perceptual law we talked about: You can't think while you focus on two or more perceptual inputs at the same time. That's the act to remember to return to. Just remember to say, 'I feel the air flowing in and out my nose.' And turn in that direction with your attention. Feel the pop as you return to the present moment and let yourself enjoy that pop!"

"That's what I love," Lisa put in, "that sudden sense of being here again, where I can breathe and relax away from my thoughts. But after a few breaths, I need to remember to say the second focus phrase or I start thinking again. It's that expansion to also feeling the movements down in my chest and belly that does the trick—two things at once!"

"And if you feel you've already blown off your emotional charge and opened up in your heart earlier in the meditation," Robert went on, "you can continue expanding your awareness of the present moment by becoming aware of a specific body part—your left foot, your right hand, your throat—and also expand to include the sounds around you. That's a very powerful expansion."

"Okay, I do all that, then what?" Dan asked.

"Then as you stay aware of the present moment, and your heart, and the world around you, it's certainly okay to have thoughts flowing through your mind again, but see if you can feel some distance between them and you. Watch them come into your mind but don't get involved with them, don't attach to them, and they'll flow right off again. That's the judo trick. And I assure you that after a while, when you don't get caught up in the thoughts, they'll start to quiet down. And of course, keep returning to the focus phrases over and over, so that you keep yourself in the present moment."

"What I find sometimes," Lisa offered, "is that several times, like Dad just said, I quiet my mind with the focus phrases and let the thoughts come. Then I get quiet again, and then there'll be a longer quiet, and then some great insight will pop into my mind as if by magic. Right out of the middle of the quiet comes this great thought that's entirely different, from some different source than my usual thoughts."

Everyone was quiet a moment.

"Okay, I think I'm getting this," Kent said. "I hear the sound of the car off in the distance, I feel the tension in my back, and the pillow under me, and the breeze blowing in through the window, and I hear the dog barking off somewhere over there, and I see Lisa's hair blowing in the breeze."

He stopped talking; everybody laughed. He'd successfully shut himself up.

~~~~~~~~~~~~~~~~~~~~

It's true, God does provide us with a built-in silencer that we can use any time we want, if only we remember to. The psychological truth is that our thoughts are almost entirely based on past experiences and ideas, and future imaginations and projections. And when we shift our focus of attention directly onto our present-moment perceptual experience, our thoughts tend to disappear, they dry up, they cease to exist in that perceptual moment.

Another reason why meditation leads to pleasure and bliss, based on another important psychological or neurological fact, is that we only experience enjoyment of life here in this present moment. Why is this? Because enjoyment is a physical, bodily experience, it's not a thought or a belief—it's a happening. After all, we only know that something is making us feel good because certain present-moment physiological happenings occur inside our bodies that we register as good feelings. Feel, after all, is something the body does; thoughts don't feel, do they?

You're liable to say, well, wait, I can think a thought, like getting an ice cream later today, and that thought will make me anticipate eating the ice cream, and that feels good. So can't thoughts make us feel good?

Still, the actual experience of feeling good when we imagine doing something we like in the future happens right here in the body in the present moment. We remember how we enjoyed ice cream in the past, and as we imagine eating ice cream in the future, our bodies actually flush with physical sensations and hormones and all the rest to generate the feeling that comes with eating an ice cream cone.

The point is this: Our bodies are where we feel. Even if we're dreaming of something in the future, it's right here in the present moment that our bodies are experiencing the good feeling. The present moment is the home of all feelings.

Unfortunately, many of us find that we don't like many of our feelings because they're worrying or depressing or confused or angry or whatever. And so to avoid our bad feelings, we develop the habit of just "not being here" most of the time, because "here" is where we feel upsetting emotions. Instead, we habitually get lost in thoughts of past and future, and this avoidance pattern does keep us from feeling our bad feelings.

The radical downside to this habit (which so many people have) is that when you habitually avoid "being here" by being lost in thoughts about the past or the future, you also lose the chance of feeling good. And the bottom line with human beings, as with other creatures on this earth, is that we like to feel good!

For every one of us with the self-defeating habit of avoiding our feelings, meditation offers a definite, safe, and healing way to break out of the habitual numbness we've made of our lives. Meditation offers a way to tune into the bad feelings, let them heal, and come out and be gone so that there's room for good feelings on a regular basis.

What we're trying to resolve in this chapter on quieting the mind, is the question of habits. Once a thinkaholic habit is established, how can we break free from it now that we're ready to get over old bad feelings and move into new good ones?

As Robert is explaining, meditation provides a step-by-step, proven structure that helps us gently approach our feelings over and over, slowly accept and resolve them, and, in the process, quiet our minds. What Kent was just describing is that very act of purposefully turning the mind's attention to as many sensory inputs in the present moment as you find appearing in your experiential world.

This is best done effortlessly, as a game. You move through the first three expansions, and then just begin to notice every new sensation that comes to you, and then every new sensation that appears—life is an unending discovery of new sensations. If you pause and watch, there's always something new coming into dominance in your mind, and then something else that is new—the present moment continues to unfold!

The amazing thing we learn in meditation is this: Not only is there always some sensory happening taking place in the present moment, but there are always more than one sensory event happening at any one moment. So we can always stay fully tuned into the present moment if we want to. That's why we start with the breathing—it's a constant sensory happening, right inside your nose and chest and belly. Likewise your heart is always beating a new beat that's never happened before. And gravity is always pulling on your body, awakening millions of tiny muscular responses that you can feel as you keep your balance. There are scents in the air, and sensations at your fingertips. There are almost always sounds around you, and certainly sights to behold.

Just try to sit and not experience any perceptual happenings—do it now, just put the book aside, move through the three focus phrases first, and then simply pay attention, one after the other, to the dominant sensory happenings occurring each new moment. Notice what happens to your thoughts as you stay attuned to the experience of the ever-new, ever-emerging present moment.

pause and experience

CHAPTER 17
Quieting Your Mind

~~~~~~~~~~~~

Robert had brought a few books with him, and he reached and opened one to a bookmark, then looked a little more and found what he was looking for.

"This fellow Krishnamurti," he said almost reverently, "who refused to be seen as the new messiah and instead chose to live a life of constant teaching of the Way, knew exactly how to express all this. He said, 'Commit your whole being, your whole energy, vitality, and passion to the entirety of life. Then we can proceed to find out what it means to meditate.' Isn't that a great statement! People think of meditation as some passive thing, but it's actually full of passion and excitement right in the middle of the peace and quiet. I bring this up because there's such a misunderstanding of what we're doing in meditation. It's not just a pacifier—just the opposite. Meditation wakes us up; it sets us free. Hold on," he said, and looked through the book again.

The others in the room sat there and met one another's glances, somewhat shyly, but said nothing. Finally Robert found what he was looking for. "Here it is, Krishnamurti again: 'Freedom is at the beginning of meditation, not the end. What is important from beginning to end is not controlling thought but understanding it, understanding the origin, the beginning of thought, which is in yourself. Thought springs from the storehouse of memory. Simply look, and see—then you are already free from thought. In meditation one has to find out whether there is an end to thought, to knowledge. There is freedom only when there is freedom from the known, because the known is the past—the present is always new, unknown.' "

Robert fell quiet, put the book down. No one said anything for a moment. Then Julie spoke up. "That guy's definitely a radical."

"You bet," Robert said.

"But I agree with him," Kent added. "As long as we're just getting programmed with ideas from the past, we're not going to be free thinkers, or free from thought as I suppose Krishnamurti would say."

"Dad has read that out loud before," Lisa said, "and what I always remember the most is the statement 'Simply look, and see— then you are already free.' That's what I get about meditation the clearest. That when we quiet our minds so we can just experience what really is, whatever it is at that moment, that's as close as we get to being free, to seeing what life is really all about."

"Okay, so we want to be free from our thoughts. So what's the fourth focus phrase about—thoughts?" Danny asked, wanting to know.

"Just that simple," Robert said. "My mind is now quiet."

"But what if I say that when my mind isn't quiet?"

"These focus phrases aren't positive affirmations trying to force something," Robert explained. "They're mind pointers. And saying 'My mind is now quiet' will aim you in the direction of a quiet mind. It actually works wonders, at least for me."

"Wait, there's something we haven't talked about," Lisa put in. "There's a special way of saying these focus phrases that makes them come alive. Rather than just saying them and being done with them, what Dad means is that we hold the sayings in our minds, and let the sayings resonate so that they fill our minds. That's what happens with me, with this fourth one especially. I say 'My mind is now quiet' and I hold that thought or that intent in my mind, and sure enough, my mind effortlessly becomes quiet, as if responding to the suggestion. Did I say that right, Dad?"

Robert grinned. "You're my guru," he joked.

Robert is obviously a serious fan of Krishnamurti, and for good reason: Krishnamurti didn't play any of the usual guru games. He was born in India around a hundred years ago, and when he was still just a little boy, a group of English and American spiritual teachers identified him as being, believe it or not, the world's next messiah, or savior, after Jesus. They basically stole him from his humble home and took him to England and then to America, where he grew up and was prepped to be the world's next spiritual savior.

But when he was a young man he stood up and, to their dismay, told his many thousands of followers "no deal." And from then on, Krishnamurti went in just the opposite direction of having people worship him, even though he was obviously in many ways an enlightened being. He insisted that no one worship anyone, that spirituality was all about equality and about looking within for the answers rather than looking to another person.

Until his death in his nineties, Krishnamurti continued to teach his radical approach to meditation, wherein we are to simply look and see directly—and know the truth of life for ourselves without any cultural assumptions or religious beliefs standing in our way.

Krishnamurti saw our chronic thought-flow as being our mental and spiritual jailors, and our ability to step back and stop identifying with our thoughts as our primary act of liberation. He didn't suggest that we try to eliminate our thoughts, just that we observe them in action, see them for what they are, and then let go of them.

And in meditation this is exactly what we do: We regularly act to bring ourselves into the present moment. And when we are in the present moment, we observe whatever thoughts continue to flow through our minds. And at some point, when we're ready to move completely into the present moment and into a direct encounter with the divine, we say "My mind is now quiet," and we move from the realm of thinking into the infinite realm of experience that comes to us, fresh and unexpected, whenever we are fully "here."

Let's move through this natural process again and notice that each time you move through this expansion of consciousness, you have a new experience, because the present is always new.

"I feel the air, flowing in and out, through my nose."

"I feel the movements in my chest and belly as I breathe."

"I'm aware of my heart right in the middle of my breathing."

"My mind is now quiet."

~~~~~~~~~~~~~~~~~~~~~~

pause and experience

CHAPTER 18

Loving Yourself—Really

As the five meditators were sitting quietly together, there came a soft knocking on the door of the room, and then the door opened to reveal Lisa's mom, Ruth. Lisa spoke right up to her.

"Mom, come on in," she said. "You know Julie and Dan. I'd like you to meet my new friend, Kent. Kent, this is Ruth."

Being a young gentleman, Kent stood up and shook hands. "We're learning how to be Buddhas," he said.

"Your entrance was well-timed," Robert said. "I was just gearing up to talk about the fifth focus phrase, and you seem to know this one the deepest. Would you maybe take over and explain a bit about the essential step of taking time to nurture your love for your own self?"

She didn't speak right up. Instead she looked around the group, meeting everyone's eyes, then she sat a moment, took a deep breath, relaxed, and took another. "Well," she began, "it's true that I love this fifth step very much. When I come to it, something special almost always happens inside me. And if this step isn't included in meditation, it's like the center stone is missing, the activation doesn't happen. What I'm talking about is taking time to look in your heart and see how you feel toward your own self. And then you take the giant positive step of accepting whatever you find in your heart so that you go ahead and love yourself just the way you are."

She paused a moment to let her words sink in. Dan was mulling something over, and finally he spoke up. "My mom is way off in a born-again church that I just can't get into," he admitted. "But we actually had a great talk last time I went to visit her, about Jesus saying 'Love your neighbor as you love yourself,' and how that's so sharp a statement because you can't really love anyone else any more than you can love yourself. I hadn't thought about that before, but as she was talking about it, it made perfect sense. But I don't have any idea how to love myself; that seems somehow a real selfish thing to spend time doing."

"It's true though," Robert put in. "And that highlights one of the special features of meditation: that we have a certain responsibility, first of all, to make sure that our own hearts and minds are healthy and open and loving. Luckily, we're naturally built so that if we only can manage to stop regularly and tune into our hearts, and make this fifth step of accepting and loving ourselves just as we are, then an amazing healing process gets activated inside us."

"This word love," Julie said, "sometimes I think it doesn't have any meaning at all anymore, it's used in commercials and political slogans and pornography and everywhere so casually that who knows what love is?"

No one spoke up after that; they all sat a moment reflecting. "Well, I know what love is," Kent risked saying. "Don't laugh at me, but a little while ago sitting here, I felt like there was so much love in the room here. It's embarrassing to say, but that's what I felt."

After another moment of quiet, Lisa said, "Jesus also said 'Love each other like I have loved you.' I remember reading somewhere about that statement, and how Jesus loved without judging anyone at all, he accepted everybody and whole, regardless of whether they were prostitutes or thieves or liars or whatever. He just let his love flow to everybody."

"My mom once complained about the way Jesus was mean to his own mother," Kent said. "I mean, he went and got himself nailed to the cross and killed, right in front of her, and broke her heart. And my mom said, 'How could he be so cruel as to make his own mother experience that unbelievable agony?' And it's true, he made all his followers go through this terrible heartbreak when he didn't really have to go into Jerusalem at all. If he'd been thinking about not hurting the feelings of the people who loved him, he wouldn't have done what he did. Which makes me think that, for him, love was doing what felt right regardless of the consequences, that we're not here just to make sure we don't cause the people around us any emotional upset. We're here to do what we have to do. Jesus was walking the heart path and he followed his heart and that's the love he's talking about, isn't it?"

"Exactly," Ruth agreed. "And I do feel that the word love carries great power even if it's misused sometimes, because all the world's religions agree that love is the center of human life, and that ultimately, God is love. That's a gigantic thing to say and maybe we never can quite grasp what love is with our thinking minds. But this fifth expansion helps us to get past ideas about love and tune into love as a feeling in our hearts. And until we just give up all our self-judging and negative attitudes about our own self-worth and so forth, we can't tune into that feeling in our hearts. So this fifth focus phrase is like magic. It turns your attention in the direction of accepting and loving yourself as if you're your own best friend."

"Okay," Dan said. "Let me guess what this next phrase must be: 'I love myself just the way I am.' Is that close?"

Lisa laughed. "Direct hit."

"But maybe when I say that, I don't really like myself at all," Dan went on. "A lot of the time I feel totally down on myself; I mean, I'm just a wreck a lot of the time."

"Jesus would love you anyway, Buddha would love you anyway. And really, what happens if you go ahead and love yourself even when you're not perfect?" Lisa asked him. "I mean, Julie isn't perfect, but you love her, don't you?"

The question made Dan a little embarrassed. "Well, yeah, sure."

"And she loves you just the way you are. So what's the problem with you loving yourself just the way you are?"

"Maybe I'd lose the drive to try to improve myself," he said.

"Well," Ruth put in, "maybe when you love yourself just as you are, that's the truly biggest improvement you can make, because when you let love flow in, everything brightens, messed-up emotions heal, and you change. Love is a power; there's no doubt about that. And as soon as you just go ahead and love yourself just as you are, you activate a cleansing process. It's hard to talk about, but you can feel it immediately when you get to this fifth expansion, and say 'I love myself just as I am,' and let those words open your heart to your own self."

Again there's a few moments of quietness in the room.

"The simple truth is," Ruth told them in her humble voice, "no one can love us if we don't love ourselves first. And we can't love other people unless we first learn to love ourselves. This is a primary challenge in life if we want to feel good in our hearts and spread love. And meditation is the tool for regularly pausing and acting in the direction of learning to love ourselves more. It's a progression like everything in meditation, every day you go deeper and deeper."

"Can we try it?" Kent asked. "And do we always start at the beginning or can we just jump right into the focus phrase we want to focus on?"

"That's a big question," Robert said. "And for me the answer is very clear. There's a progression in meditation, and each time you find that you've dropped out of a meditative state into thoughts, it's important to go back to the beginning, to your breathing, because that's really the entry door, the portal that opens your experience to the next steps. You tune into your breathing experience, come fully into the present moment, then

look to your heart to release pent-up emotions. Next you quiet your mind, and in this expanded state you're ready to say the fifth focus phrase and open your heart to accept and love yourself just as you are. And that, of course, leads to the sixth focus phrase that we'll get to next. Does anybody need to go anywhere, or do we have time to go all the way through, maybe another half an hour?"

Everyone wanted to continue and it was only five o'clock, so they took time to move through the first five expansions in meditation, as Robert said, quietly, with plenty of time in between:

"I feel the air, flowing in and out, through my nose."

"I feel the movements in my chest and belly as I breathe."

"I'm aware of my heart right in the middle of my breathing."

"My mind is now quiet."

"I love myself just as I am."

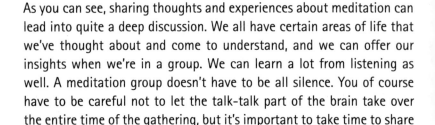

As you can see, sharing thoughts and experiences about meditation can lead into quite a deep discussion. We all have certain areas of life that we've thought about and come to understand, and we can offer our insights when we're in a group. We can learn a lot from listening as well. A meditation group doesn't have to be all silence. You of course have to be careful not to let the talk-talk part of the brain take over the entire time of the gathering, but it's important to take time to share your experiences and insights, and also your questions and doubts, with your friends.

The issue of love is best approached by remembering that love is not an idea, not a conceptual understanding. Love is an experience that is felt most strongly in the heart. We've seen that the heart is actually a fifth brain, and when we consider the power of the heart to both receive and broadcast love, we enter into an amazing realm of human experience that takes us ultimately into direct communion with God, with the infinite wisdom and compassion that in truth sustains the universe.

What is it that keeps us from feeling love in our hearts all the time? You might want to contemplate this question a number of times as you go deeper into the answer. Let me give you some beginning guidelines, and then you can reflect on your own understanding of the dynamic of love in your life.

Whether we turn to Lao Tzu in the Chinese Taoist tradition, to Buddha and Patanjali in the Buddhist and Hindu traditions, to Jesus in the Christian tradition, or to Muhammad in the Muslim tradition—wherever we look for deep insight into love, we find all the great teachers saying the same thing: "Fear not." From a psychological point of view, we cannot be in fear, and in love, at the same time. When we're anxious or worried, or feeling related emotions such as aggression or depression or confusion, we lose touch with our hearts because we've dropped down into the more reflexive reptilian areas of the brain where compassion simply doesn't exist.

Love is a quality of emotion where we accept the world just as it is, even unto death. And in fact, our fear of our own demise is the underlying fear from which all other fears emerge. So if we want to truly live a life of love, we need to deal with our chronic worries, our underlying apprehensions, and ultimately our fear of our own inevitable death. I give you this challenge: Every time you find yourself feeling anxious or worried or otherwise heavy and closed down in your heart, look directly at that feeling. Catch fear in action and notice what happens when you tune into your heart, come into the present moment, and let love flow in again.

As we've noted already, fear is a past-future function of the mind (unless, of course, the lion is charging you in the present moment, in which case you react instantly and worry about it later). Love, on the other hand, is a feeling in the heart in the present moment. So these tools you're learning in meditation—to shift from past-future into the present moment by tuning into your breathing and so forth in the here and now—can be used anywhere and at anytime to shift out of anxiety and into love.

Again, let's put it all together, and practice—and experience directly.

"I feel the air, flowing in and out, through my nose."

"I feel the movements in my chest and belly as I breathe."

"I'm aware of my heart right in the middle of my breathing."

"My mind is now quiet."

"I love myself just as I am."

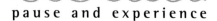

pause and experience

After ten minutes or so of meditating, Ruth's eyes opened and she found Robert looking at her. She smiled softly in response to the love she saw in his eyes, and then she looked at the four youthful meditators, all of them with their eyes still closed. She let them meditate a few moments longer, then reached over to a shelf that held a small gong and mallet. She took a deep breath, then tapped the gong softly. The sound brought eyes opening here and there, until everyone was quietly awaiting her next words.

"Maybe it seems that with that fifth expansion," she said, "we've reached the final expansion, with love in our hearts. If there exists no deeper spiritual dimension in life, this would be true, and I don't mean to push my belief, my personal experience, that there is more to life than our three-dimensional scientific reality. But for me there is more, and we can discover for ourselves that this is true, in meditation, and in the sixth expansion."

She paused as a sudden gust of wind came blowing through the window and through the room. The weather was changing. Lisa stood up and went to close the window halfway. When she was sitting again, Ruth went on. "Once we've stopped judging ourselves and the world around us, and have experienced our own capacity to love," she told them, "we're ready to go on to the next step, which is to open our hearts and minds and souls to the inflow of love and insight from beyond our personal biological centers. We're ready to open up and receive God's love, directly, with no priests or theologies standing between us and the ultimate reality."

"Yipes," Danny said. "That sounds pretty scary. I mean, don't they say that if you look directly at God, you'll go blind or something?"

"Well, who is it that says that kind of fear-based thing?" she asked.

"Hmm . . . priests."

"I don't mean to talk down the calling of being a priest," she explained. "There are a great many priests and ministers and shamans doing their best to lead people in the same direction we're pointing here, toward intimate contact with God. The problem with priests is that when they stand between us and God, they gain great power, and power tends to corrupt. But I say, anyone who says we can't turn our focus of attention toward God directly hasn't meditated, or they'd know that it's the opposite of dangerous. It's the experience of being touched by divine love. And that's the love that really heals, that's the love that brings us flashes of insight about what to do with our lives. That's what Muhammad was talking about when he said we have only to open to Allah's divine guidance in our lives, and let God's love fill us, and our lives will be happy and fulfilled."

"Uh," Dan said somewhat uncertainly, "somehow every time you say that word God I find my mind putting up its defenses. Maybe I don't want to open up to the God I've always heard about, the hell-and-brimstone God who throws nonbelievers into eternal hellfire and damnation and all the rest."

Robert nodded. "I can relate to that," he said. "Sometimes even the highest, seemingly perfect terms, like God, become concepts in our minds that separate us from the actual experience of God."

"Such a key point," Ruth added. "And when we come to this sixth expansion, it's important that you feel total freedom to change the words to match your own feelings about the divine. And maybe even the word divine doesn't work for you. All the religious words in our vocabulary are colored by the meanings that

140

particular groups have put to them. And really in meditation, we're aiming to get beyond words altogether, so we encounter the actual experience of what's real behind the words. God isn't an idea, Allah isn't a concept, Krishna isn't a logical symbol found in our thinking minds. By whatever name, the Creator permeates all of creation and can't be stuffed into any concept. We use the words here to point beyond the words. If God works for you, use that word. Or use any other word you want to. Or don't use any word at all, just say "My heart is open to receive."

"Often, for me," Lisa put in, "what I want to receive when I get to this stage of the meditation is just some insight into what I should do. And when I say 'My heart is open to receive,' I find myself opening up to what I call wisdom, or inspiration. And I don't have to give a label to the source of that insight or wisdom."

Robert smiled to her. "Thanks, Lisa. Especially for bringing up the word wisdom, because this is indeed where wisdom comes flowing in. And what's important to notice is that wisdom doesn't come from the head, it comes from the heart speaking to us."

"Uh, I'm going to have to leave in a few minutes," Kent put in. "Can we find out about the sixth expansion before I go?"

"Sure," Ruth said. "Lisa, do you want to guide us through this one? You always say it's your favorite."

"Well, okay," she said. "You can guess what it is: 'My heart is open to receive God's healing help.' I like to say the first part, 'My heart is open,' on the first breath, and then the second part, 'to receive,' on the second breath, and 'God's healing help' on the third breath. And the third part can be whatever you want at the moment, 'God's healing help' or maybe just 'healing love' or whatever you want to receive from the infinite source. The thing I find amazing is just that act of saying 'My heart is open to receive.' Every time I get to this point in the meditation, and say that, something does open inside me that tends to get closed otherwise. And I feel my heart opening. I can't describe it, but I love it. It's

like tuning into myself beyond my usual sense of who I am. And like they say, it's always new. Want to try it?"

"Yes," from the whole group.

"Okay, let's start at the beginning, and you can move fairly quickly through the first five steps, and then stay in the sixth. We'll get to the seventh step maybe next time. Here we go:

"I feel the air, flowing in and out, through my nose."

"I feel the movements in my chest and belly as I breathe."

"I'm aware of my heart right in the middle of my breathing."

"My mind is now quiet."

"I love myself just as I am."

"My heart is open to receive God's healing help."

We've now come to that remarkable place in meditation where words tend to fall completely away. We've moved through the five steps that prepare us for the ultimate meditative act of opening up to receive whatever spiritual inflow is naturally coming to us in this unique new moment. The experience is never the same. All we can say is that when we take responsibility for our own spiritual well-being, and choose to consciously open our hearts to God by whatever name, we have fully done what we can to open up to realities beyond our minds—to the infinite divine creative loving force of the universe and beyond.

My role here is not to tell you what to expect, but to assure you that if your intent is to open up to God, and if you state this intent clearly with your own mind, that this is what you'll experience, step by step—yourself unified with your creator. Meditation is the bridge between our biological consciousness and the greater consciousness. And the sixth focus phrase is the final rung in the ladder that lifts us into the light.

Of course, when you first begin experimenting with the meditational tools you're learning to use in this book, your everyday mind is going to limit how much you open your heart and mind and soul in meditation. Don't be discouraged if at first your thoughts and expectations hold the door mostly closed. Spiritual awakening, as we're approaching it here at least, is the safe secure way; it's a progressive experience, a lifetime of exploration. All you need to do is remember to move through the six steps over and over, and I assure you, lights will start to shine!

Right now you have an entire host of assumptions about what life is all about, most of them coming from your culture. We live in a very materialistic society that worships science and is highly skeptical of anything beyond what science can measure. A lot of this skepticism has been valid, because in olden days there was so much superstition and fear-based religious programming about evil forces and so forth. Thankfully we're moving beyond fear-based superstitions about the infinite reality beyond our usual senses.

At the same time, our scientific as well as our superstitious beliefs will tend to try to limit our opening to the infinite. What to do? First of all, remember not to judge yourself when you find that you feel closed to the sixth expansion. Just keep leading yourself through the focus phrases and bringing yourself to the point of opening. If you do this, then each time you'll find that you tend to open further.

Also, you'll find that it probably takes a while for you to truly trust the source of the inflow that you tap in meditation. This is natural, and to be expected. Again, don't judge yourself for this hesitation in trusting the unknown. Your ego isn't your enemy; it's there to protect you. If you allow your ego to speak the focus phrases and guide you to the point of exploration, then the ego function of the mind will be there with you—experiencing and discovering, step by step, that opening to God is always good; that allowing infinite love and wisdom to flow into your personal energy system is always wonderful and healing and helpful.

So enjoy each of the expansions every time you move through them. Go ahead and move through them a number of times in one meditation if you want to, and each time you come to the sixth expansion, just relax and see what comes. Spiritual awakening is often very subtle, and until we learn to really live in our hearts, we often are mostly numb to the experience that comes to us, because it comes through our hearts, and then up to our usual consciousness. That's why it's so important to regularly exercise your ability to tune into your heart.

Enough said for now. Let's move through this entire process again, at your own pace. And remember that every time you have your mind say the focus phrases, something happens: learning takes place, exploration widens your sense of what life is all about, and your contact with the divine, by whatever name, expands and awakens your sense of who you are as a spiritual being.

MEDITATION THREE
Quiet Mind/Open Heart

Let's move through the six meditation expansions that we've learned thus far, taking special time to explore the last three.

To begin, give yourself at least five minutes or so with nothing to do. Sit comfortably, or lie on your back if you want to, and take the time to let your body move and stretch, set your body free, give yourself permission to do whatever you want movement-wise until you find a comfortable position and posture. Go ahead and make sounds to blow off steam; yawn or do whatever else comes naturally as you settle down.

Now, begin to gently turn your mind's focus of attention toward your breathing. Notice the sensations of the air rushing in, and then rushing out, of your nose or mouth as your breaths come and go, let your breathing stop when it wants to, and start again when it wants to.

You can let your eyes close whenever they want to. Begin to also feel, from the inside out, the movements happening in your chest and belly as you breathe. Be aware of two happenings at once—in your nose, and in your chest and belly.

Now you can let your awareness expand to also include your heart, beating right in the middle of your breathing. Tune into what feelings you have deep within you and let those feelings be expressed by your breathing. With every inhale fill yourself with your emotions, with every exhale go ahead and blow those feelings out of you so that with every breath you're tuning into your whole range of feelings, letting them come flowing out of you as you breathe.

Be sure to relax your tongue, your jaw, so that your throat is relaxed. Make any sounds you want to release the tension you might find in your throat. Breathe through your mouth if you feel under pressure inside.

Now, if you're ready, begin to let your breathing calm down, to naturally become smoother. Let your inhales be the same length and depth as your exhales; allow a natural balance to begin to grow within you as your inhales and exhales become smooth and even.

For a few breaths, just watch whatever thoughts might still be flowing through your mind. Don't judge these thoughts as good or bad. Don't attach yourself to them. Just be the observer and watch your thoughts come and go.

As thoughts flow through your mind, be sure to stay aware, also, of your breathing here in the present moment, with your thoughts coming and going, and watch those thoughts as you breathe.

When you're ready, let your thoughts begin to quiet down. Focus your whole attention to your breathing, your heart, your hands, your feet, your head, your whole body, here in this present moment, and the sounds around you.

As you continue being aware of your whole body and the sounds around you, let yourself enjoy the feeling of right now, of having nothing to do, nowhere to go. Everything right now is okay and you have the time and space to just relax, to quiet your mind, open your heart and feel good inside as the breaths come and go.

Now focus again on your heart, and say to yourself: "I love myself just as I am."

Just relax, accept, and allow good feelings to fill your heart, toward yourself and those around you.

Breathing . . . heart . . . acceptance . . . love.

Now, to open up to deeper contact with divine love, wisdom, and healing, say to yourself: "My heart is open to receive God's healing help."

Just relax, open up. Let the love come flowing in, and if you want, let's go again through the process:

"I feel the air, flowing in and out, through my nose."

"I feel the movements in my chest and belly as I breathe."

"I'm aware of my heart right in the middle of my breathing."

"My mind is now quiet."

"I love myself just as I am."

"My heart is open to receive God's healing help."

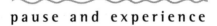

pause and experience

Part Four
SELF-AWARENESS
(Overcoming Obstacles)

In this final section, we round off the learning process, and also the story we've been following, as we learn the last of the seven meditative focus phrases and watch the people in our story come together as friends.

In our story, we see the teenagers and their parents alike struggling with the usual worries, and also learning to be more open, to share their feelings, resolve old judgments and conflicts, and live in their hearts just as much as in their minds. Especially, we see how letting go of chronic judging of oneself and other people can awaken an entirely new sense of freedom and pleasure in life.

There are always obstacles that now and then appear on the meditative path, and this section offers both inspiration and specific guidance in overcoming the obstacles and going deeper and deeper into the discovery of who you really are. In both the drama and the reflection parts of these chapters, you'll see that everyone's human, everyone's got problems and challenges in life, and everyone ultimately can employ the practical tools of self-reflection and meditation to resolve those problems and challenges.

Most important, each of us can learn to love ourselves more, so that we in turn can love others more fully. The seven focus phrases that make up the heart of this meditation program are specifically designed to lead you to the point of opening your heart to your own self as you put away judgments, quiet your busy mind, and tune into good feelings in your heart.

A special focus of this section deals with the parents of the teenagers, as the youngsters discover a good thing and, step by step, are pleased to see their parents recognizing positive change and wanting to learn what meditation is all about, too. Meditation is wonderful when done on your own, but it's also wonderful when you and your friends can come together as a group and share the insights and good feelings that emerge in meditation.

The day of the barbecue arrived and Dan found himself getting more and more nervous as the day progressed. He had a Ping-Pong tournament in the morning that Julie came to and he placed third when he was expected to take number one. He watched all sorts of negative thoughts about not being any good hit at him, trying to knock him down. He also caught himself starting to blame Julie for being there, for jinxing him.

Afterward they went out for a hamburger. She got a vegetarian burger and as they sat eating, part of him felt guilty for eating some poor suffering cow and part of him felt angry that Julie was laying her holier-than-thou trip on him. Basically, he was a wreck by the time they left the restaurant.

She took his hand but he pulled away and walked ahead of her down the shady street toward their neighborhood. She stared at him, caught herself reacting with all sorts of negative thoughts about how he was too moody to have a relationship with, and then about how she probably was the cause of his grouchiness because maybe she'd put him off his game that morning. Or maybe it was because she'd joked about finally getting to meet his dad after all this time and he'd reacted to that.

But she could see that all these thoughts could easily be exaggerated or just plain wrong. What she knew was that he was upset and she loved him and she wasn't going to let her own thoughts ruin their relationship. So she got brave and hurried to catch up to him, and pulled him to a stop.

"Danny, please," she said.

He stood there breathing hard, upset, not saying anything, just silently glowering at her.

"I've got all sorts of thoughts messing up how I feel," she admitted. "Probably you do, too. And we're feeling miserable as a result. Let's try, together," she offered, "and see if we can just pull ourselves out of this. I'll tell you what I've been thinking and you can tell me if I'm right or not, and maybe you'll do the same thing with me, okay?"

For a long moment he almost reacted and walked away, but he could feel the risk she was taking, and he could see the love in her eyes for him, and he sighed and decided to trust her. "Okay, what the hell," he said. "I'm just a mess inside today."

"It's like the present moment collapses inside my chest and I can hardly breathe," she admitted. "Like everything we've been learning with Lisa and her parents just disappear and I'm right back where I was before I started meditating. It's scary, how I can just lose it all sometimes."

"Me too. Just blank."

"I can hardly turn my mind to remember the focus phrases," she said.

"When it all feels hopeless, it seems it's not worth of remembering," he admitted, at least finding that he could talk a little about his feelings even while in the middle of them.

"Okay, let's see what you think is hopeless," she encouraged.

"Jeez, everything. I mean I failed at Ping-Pong, I've got a dad who's probably going to ruin the barbecue, I'm being depressed and mean to my girlfriend, and on top of it all, I just ate some miserable poor old cow."

He came to an end and stood there staring blankly a moment; she did, too. But then she couldn't help herself, and she burst out laughing. And just a moment later, so did Danny.

"I mean," she said through her laughter, "you're a great Ping-Pong player and nobody wins all the time and you know it, and

on top of that your dad's behavior isn't going to change how I feel about you, nor how my parents do either. And you're standing here really trying to work this through with me, and you're not being mean at all. And as for the cow, all I can say is what Lisa and Ruth were saying a few days ago: What if you just love yourself for how you are? I certainly wasn't judging you. I just don't like the taste of meat sometimes. So here we are. And my thoughts were just as stupid. I can't even remember what they were. God, I feel better!"

"I know I lost that last game this morning because, right in the middle of it, I suddenly was worrying about my dad and the barbecue. Dumb."

"And you were telling me just last night that your dad is doing better these days anyway."

"Yeah, but who knows."

"So the future grabs us again."

"Yeah. Hey, thanks. I was just totally caught up."

"Well, what are friends for anyway?"

He looked at her intently. "You really are my friend, aren't you?" he said, almost not able to believe it.

"Heart and soul," she said softly.

They walked on hand in hand through the afternoon shade.

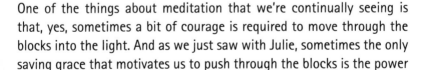

One of the things about meditation that we're continually seeing is that, yes, sometimes a bit of courage is required to move through the blocks into the light. And as we just saw with Julie, sometimes the only saving grace that motivates us to push through the blocks is the power of love itself.

This applies not only to our love for others but of course our love for ourselves as well. If we really love ourselves, we naturally don't want to see ourselves caught in emotional suffering. Maybe it takes some bravery to push through like Julie did, and Danny, too, and confront whatever's making us feel bad. But that's what life is all about: being brave enough to really live it!

One of the strange things about life is that no matter what we do or how far we advance on a spiritual path, the bugaboo of doubt still rises up to grab us. Therefore it's important to get to know doubt very well, even to make friends with it, rather than trying to reject it.

One of the biggest lessons of love is that we tend to love what is beautiful and healthy and bright, and reject what is ugly and sick and dark. Yet the truth of the matter is this: The main things in life that really need some loving attention are precisely those things we usually reject. Jesus and Buddha didn't go around just loving the nice sweet good people around them. They especially had compassion on those who were suffering and angry and depressed and confused and hurting.

Julie was able to love Dan's upset and almost ugly side. Her love shining on that part of him and accepting that part of him was a major factor in his being able to look at his own pains and confusions, and turn some of his own loving (and humorous) attention their way. In the process, he helped to heal those needy parts of his psyche.

Who really needs your loving attention today?

And are you grounded enough in your love for yourself to have some extra to share with someone who really needs a bit of extra love— to help heal, get clear, and open their own heart again?

Meditation is a primary way to regularly pause, shine loving attention on your own hurts and wounds, and then let love flow in to fill your heart so that you can go out into the world and let your light shine on those around you.

Imagine if all of us just took ten minutes each morning before going to school or out into the world to recharge our love batteries so that we had some extra love to share with those around us? What a wonderful world it would be, and even if no one else is doing it, at least you can be a bright light.

And then, when you're caught in an episode of doubt, perhaps someone you helped brighten up earlier will come by and give you some loving attention, too.

Remember that giving love isn't something your ego does, it's not something you do in order to get something back. Giving love is something you do because it feels good to let the love flow. When we get stuck in doubt and depression and confusion, chances are high there's no love flowing through our hearts right then—and no wonder we feel terrible. A heart without love is the worst torture there is.

So when you're caught in doubt and feel down on yourself, what can you do? First of all, like Danny and Julie did, do your best to at least watch the thoughts that are making you feel bad. Catch them in the act and challenge them. Are they true? Or are they just a product of self-doubt and negative mental habits?

Another thing to do, again seen in what Julie and Danny did, is to get the thoughts verbalized and out in the open where they can be seen for what they really are. Express the thoughts that are dragging you down and chances are they'll get caught in the light of rational truth and dissolve into thin air. "It's not as bad as you think it is" is so often the case when we feel depressed and caught up in self-doubt.

The other thing about self-doubt and depression is that time does heal. If you can just ride through the dark period, stay as much in the present moment as you can, and let your emotions flow out on every new exhale, the darkness will pass and the fog will lift. Something will happen that will help to pull you out of your negative thoughts about life and back into the flow of the present moment where you can feel alive again.

And throughout any bummer period when you're down and out, do your best to remember that all you have to do is say that first statement to yourself that will focus your attention to the air flowing in and out your nose or mouth as you breathe . . . and just hold your mind on that focus phrase until you remember the next phrase, which will aim your mind's attention to the movements in your chest and belly as you breathe . . . and follow this spiritual lifeline as you remember to tune into the presence of your heart, right in the middle of your breathing—go ahead and blow off your emotions with every new exhale . . . and then remember to allow your mind to be quiet of all those upsetting thoughts . . . and then just go ahead and accept yourself just as you are, with all your upset feelings and let the love flow in . . . until you reach the point where you remember to open your heart to the healing power of love that comes flowing into your heart from that infinite source of love. Let the healing happen.

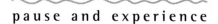

pause and experience

CHAPTER 21

Having Faith in Your Practice

Julie helped her mom prepare for the barbecue, making potato salad all on her own as her mom made the tossed green salad and a dip plate of sliced vegetables.

"It's strange to have so many people over who I don't know at all," her mom said, exhaling with a nervous sigh at the thought of the busy get-together. "Let's see, there's your friend Lisa and her parents, and this fellow Kent and his parents, and Danny and his parents—"

"Both Kent and Danny are parent singular, I told you," Julie said impatiently.

"Whatever, that's seven, eight people I don't know. Peter gets these big ideas."

"It'll be fun," Julie encouraged.

"You're getting pretty serious about Danny, it seems."

"Is that a problem? It's not like we're going to run off and get married tomorrow. He's my friend. My best friend."

"No, it's not a problem. I'm just nervous. I just don't know what to expect with people I don't know; it makes me nervous just thinking about tonight."

"Well then, maybe you might ask Lisa to teach you some meditation that'll help you not get nervous about the future so much," Julie said with impatience in her voice. She was just beginning to notice that her own nerves weren't as calm as she'd like them to be, and that she was snipping at her mom unfairly.

Her mom stood at the counter with her paring knife raised in the air, staring out the window. "What? Do you think it would actually help?" she asked her daughter.

Julie was surprised. "Well, it's helped me, no question about that," she said. "And don't mention that I said this, but Kent's mother suffers sometimes from depression and I think he wants her to talk to Lisa's parents, maybe see if they might start a parent meditation class, something like that."

"Oh?"

"What? You actually might be interested?"

"Well," her mom said, "I don't want this to sound like I wasn't liking you before, but the truth is you're easier to get along with. We don't argue so much since you started meditating. But what was that about depression?"

"Just that meditation sometimes helps, a lot, with it."

"I would have thought that sitting around mulling over your problems in meditation would just make it worse, not better. I've always done my best to keep active and outgoing rather than sink any deeper into my, my . . ."

"Mom, meditation isn't mulling over problems, it's quieting the thoughts that are the cause of the problem."

"Well, anyway, all this stress with so many people coming . . . go ask your father if he needs help, would you? You know how he gets lackadaisical right when I need him to get in gear."

Julie heard in her mother's voice that recurrent edge of judgment that brought on so many of the family fights. "That right there is something that meditation would help you look at," Julie was brave enough to say. "You have this whole set of reasons why you aren't satisfied with Daddy. What would happen if you just accepted him the way he is, like I do Danny, and stopped judging him as less than what you require?"

The question caught her mom halfway through an inhale, and she stood there just staring at her daughter a moment. "But that's not fair, I don't judge him, there are simply certain things that he doesn't—"

"But that's judgment, Mom. Really, what would happen if you just let go of all your judging and pushing, and let Dad be who he naturally is?"

"I'll tell you what would happen, this whole household would just slow down and fall apart, that's what."

"Well, maybe I'd prefer that to all your arguing and not accepting him the way he is—and him the same with you. That's what I'm learning in meditation, that the first step toward world peace is for each of us to accept each other. Jesus and Buddha taught that real love doesn't judge, that there's another way to live life besides fighting against the way things are. Dad's just Dad. I guess I do wish you would learn how to meditate, maybe from Lisa's parents. I think it would help heal this whole household. If we all just had faith that everything would work out okay if everyone was allowed to be their natural self, I think things would be a lot better around here."

Her mother stood there somewhat aghast at what she'd just been told. And Julie, for her part, surprised at her outburst, turned quickly and walked out of the kitchen and into the cooling afternoon air, feeling hot with a passion that had actually felt just perfect to let come out finally. She hoped she hadn't hurt her mom's feelings, but on the other hand she'd said what she felt from the heart was true, and wasn't that what being real was all about?

Well, on the other hand, her mother's assumption about her husband had been true: He'd hardly made any progress with the barbecue; he hadn't even cleaned the grill yet. Instead, he was sitting under the big shade tree, enjoying the afternoon breeze, petting the dog, sipping a beer, and listening on his new outdoor speakers to an old recording of Miles Davis that he just loved.

Julie stood a moment watching him from behind his back, wondering if what she'd said to her mom was really true: would the world still work okay if everyone got to just be who they naturally were, like Lao Tzu and the Taoists had recommended? Wouldn't some people end up doing all the work, while others would just be sitting around and enjoying life? On the other hand, Julie remembered how her mom was almost entirely unable to just kick back and relax like her dad could. Maybe if she relaxed more he'd get into gear more.

Lured by the peace of the afternoon, Julie went over and sat down beside her father on the lawn chairs, put her feet up on the table even though she knew her mother would complain if she saw, and accepted a sip of her father's beer. It tasted awful but she didn't let on.

"Maybe we should get things in gear soon," she said after a few minutes of Miles Davis and the mellow jazz riffs of his "Sketches of Spain," feeling her own rising desire to go into action for the barbecue. "Mom's worried the guests will come and we won't be ready."

He scowled. "I try to tell her there's no need to worry, we have all afternoon, she's just concerned about what people will think if we're not the perfect hosts. Well, this is my only day to relax, and relax is what I'm doing. She's such a worry wart," he complained.

"Maybe that's just her," Lisa said.

Her father looked at her. "Yeah, I know. And she's got her good sides, too, obviously."

The jazz trumpet played on until suddenly out of the blue, Lisa thought of Danny and his father probably on their way right now to the barbecue. She felt her breathing get gripped with excitement and also apprehension, her body charged with energy, and also shaky with uncertainty. She tried to calm down; she went through the six steps she'd learned in meditation, but she was so impatient she lost track of the focus phrases halfway through as her mind remembered that the grill needed cleaning.

Just to give herself something to do so that she didn't go crazy, *she got up and cleaned the whole barbecue area vigorously. She found that the action calmed her down. She felt the sensation of her bare feet on the red bricks, the breeze picking up again, the birds singing in the three trees farther back in the yard, the scent in the air. All of a sudden she realized that her senses had brought her into the present moment and helped her let go of her apprehensions—and that was meditation as well. Aha, she thought with a bit of humor. Maybe I'm going to be a Buddha some day, after all. Let's see, which tree shall I go sit under to await the flash of enlightenment?*

It's so important to allow inner growth and insights, to expand and touch the hearts of those around us. One of the great lessons of meditation is that honesty and speaking from the heart is the best way to move through life. Julie, for instance, let herself break free and speak from the heart when she told her mom what she really felt. And what are the consequences of truly speaking from the heart? In many ways, the outcome of such a passionate outburst depends on whether there are angry and judgmental feelings behind the spontaneous expression, or if the words come truly from a place of compassion and honesty.

In Julie's case, what she let come out into the open was something she'd recently been thinking about a lot, regarding her parents. She'd already felt in her heart that her feelings were valid, so she trusted, had faith, and let them come out into the open. It's always a risk to speak from the heart. But otherwise, as they say, "Nothing ventured, nothing gained, and nothing still remains." On the other hand, the more we risk speaking from the heart, like Julie had earlier that afternoon with Danny, and again with her mother, the more we can see the fruits of being honest.

From her conversations with Lisa, Julie had taken to heart how Jesus had set a strong example not of trying to avoid hurting people's feelings but rather of always doing what feels right in spite of how others might react—and of trusting that honesty is never ultimately damaging. Lisa had mentioned several times how Jesus had said "Know the truth, and the truth will set you free," and that's just how Julie felt as she walked over to her father as he sat near the barbecue. She felt free of a heavy burden; she had told her mother what she honestly felt, and her mother could do what she wanted with the information.

Julie's experience with her mom demonstrates one of the definite rules of meditation: The more you practice being honest, the more it becomes a part of you that begins to just happen naturally on its own. Likewise, the more you practice shifting into the present moment, the easier that shift is going to become, until you reach that point where it begins happening on its own.

The truth is, that special mental state we enter in meditation isn't something unusual or different from normal human consciousness. A good true meditation program wisely takes its design from the natural way the human mind effortlessly functions when it isn't gripped with upsetting thoughts and memories and fantasies. Each time we pause and look at a sunset and enter into that deep blissful meditative experience, this is surely a natural process. Same with when we get carried away listening to music and experience a mini-rapture.

When approached clearly and without ulterior motives, meditation is exercise for the mental muscle that enables us to move our focus of attention toward the present moment whenever we want to. And definitely, the better we get to know that special place or feeling that we enter when we quiet our thoughts and focus on the unfolding of the eternal present, the easier it becomes to find that expanded consciousness.

Our lifelong meditative aim (if we can even talk about an aim in meditation) is surely to spend more and more time in that expanded consciousness where we're more alive, more responsive, more loving, and even wise. And you can trust your new meditative practice to regularly aim you toward that expanded consciousness.

Let's pause yet again to move through the basic inner process that leads us into perfect position for opening our hearts and receiving. Just make the decision that you're going to move through the seven expansions of meditation, and then let the focus phrases point your mind where you want it to go.

"I feel the air, flowing in and out, through my nose."

"I feel the movements in my chest and belly as I breathe."

"I'm aware of my heart right in the middle of my breathing."

"My mind is now quiet"

"I love myself just as I am."

"My heart is open to receive God's healing help."

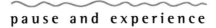

pause and experience

CHAPTER 22
Letting Go of Judgment

The beautiful here-and-now mood Julie had slipped into as she prepared the outside cooking area for the barbecue was popped the moment she heard her mother talking to someone inside the house.

"Daddy," she said urgently, putting a hand on his shoulder. "Please remember to be extra nice to Danny's dad, okay?"

Her father stood up, having noticed the sudden worry in Julie's voice and expression. "Sure," he said. "I mean, the whole point here is to get along. Besides, Dan's a great guy; his father's bound to have some good points. Oh, and hey, thanks for getting things ready. I was going to, you know that, but just in my own time."

The back screen door opened and sure enough, there was Danny with a tall, strong-looking and really handsome man who must be his father. Julie couldn't help herself; she went running eagerly across the lawn and up to them, taking Danny's hand without even thinking about it.

"Uh, meet my pops, George," Danny said a bit awkwardly.

Julie felt a sudden burst of confidence as she extended her hand and met this man's eyes. "A pleasure," she said. "Come and meet my dad."

Both Danny and Julie stood watching as the two fathers shook hands and started chatting. George noticed the clever latticework that her father had done, and commented on it—and the two men went off talking nonstop about carpentry, sipping their beers and enjoying the ongoing mellow jazz.

Julie led Danny inside rather than stand around watching the old folk, and as they came into the living room Kent and his mother came in, together with Lisa and her parents. Wow, thought Julie, looking for the first time at Kent's mother, she's gorgeous.

The afternoon dwindled toward dusk as chips and dips were consumed, and then hamburgers and steaks and fish were grilled. Lisa's parents, who didn't eat meat, had brought some tofu steaks that they had marinated and were ready to barbecue on the grill, along with some veggies. George made some joking comment on now having seen everything, but he wasn't putting anybody down, and as Danny noticed, he wasn't getting drunk. What he was doing the last half-hour was talking enjoyably with Veronica, Kent's mom. They seemed to be getting along well together.

In fact everyone was having a great time, Julie thought; the party was a big success, but no, where was her mother? She hadn't come out at all to grab anything to eat. Feeling a pang of uncertainty, Julie excused herself and went into the house.

She found her mother in the bedroom, just sitting there, looking like maybe she'd been crying. "Mom," Julie said, coming over to her. "What's wrong, did I upset you with what I said earlier? I'm sorry."

Her mom was silent a long time. Then she said, "It's not your fault. It's just that, deep down, you're right. We both know your dad's a wonderful human being. Why can't I just let him be the way he is? If he was different maybe I wouldn't even want to be with him. He calms me down, he always has. And what do I do? I complain about him being so calm. I'm terrible. I don't deserve his love, or yours."

Julie had known her mother to slip into these dark moods often, but this time Julie didn't respond like she usually did. Instead of anxiously trying to boost her mom's morale, she just sat on the bed with her a moment, letting her mother have her feelings, and just be how she was right then.

"You know, Mom," she finally said, "it's true that neither of you are perfect. But really, who's to judge? I love you both, just the way you are. I only wish you didn't have to be so unhappy inside. And from what I'm learning, I think the main cause of your upsets is that you're always thinking about not being good enough—either you're putting Dad down, or you're putting yourself down. What we're learning in meditation is that the dumbest thing we can do is to judge ourselves. It's like hitting ourselves over the head with a hammer, as Robert puts it. What would happen if you decided to stop judging the world, and just accepted reality the way it is?"

"Oh, I don't think I could," she answered.

"Would you be willing to try?"

"What? You mean learn to meditate?"

"It's not just meditation," Julie said, "it's an entirely more heartful way to go about life. The way Robert says it: Rather than letting your thoughts torture you, you decide to take control of your mind and stop the torture."

"But I've tried to do that all my life."

"Well, maybe you just didn't have the right tools. Anyway, it's just a suggestion. Come on, why don't we go outside and eat."

Her mom sighed, then stood up. She turned to Julie with tears in her eyes. "What did I do to deserve such a wonderful daughter?" she said sincerely.

"Well," Julie said, a playful glint appearing in her eyes, "maybe all you did was act naturally, and here I am, and here you are. Who knows what might come next. What I want is another burger!"

~~~~~~~~~~~~~~

Julie does know what she wants to have happen: She wants her mother to learn how to run her mind so that she doesn't suffer. She wants her to learn to meditate, and hopefully become happier and less judgmental as a result. Do you think Julie's being selfish in this desire, pushing her mother to do something maybe her mom doesn't want? Or is it perfectly fine and even a loving act to encourage someone to look into meditation?

This raises the whole issue of where to draw the line between wanting to help someone and interfering with his or her life. One of the primary things we learn in meditation is that it's best to stay out of trying to influence other people's spiritual lives. Meditation is not an evangelistic movement. We do not assume responsibility for other people's salvation or anything like that. If we're accepting the people around us just as they are, we can express our enthusiasm for meditation and its benefits, but we don't pressure them into joining our club. From a meditation perspective, we're all individually responsible for our own lives. We are in no way responsible for other people's lives. Therefore we do best to accept and love, and stay out of other people's spiritual decisions as much as possible. Our responsibility is to focus on doing all we can to live our own lives as best we can, so that we naturally radiate, by example, the loving benefits of an inner spiritual meditative path.

This can't be said often enough: Love means accepting other people just the way they are, rather than expecting them to change so that they fit our image of how we want them to be. Julie's mom, like so many people, suffers because she can't accept other people just as they are. She lives in a fear-based world where nothing is good enough, where there's a constant anxious battle between the way the world is and the way she thinks it needs to change to be acceptable.

If she learns to meditate, and therefore to look deeply into this judgmental part of her personality, what she's almost certainly going to find is that the main person she doesn't accept is her own self. And once she realizes that she's judging herself as not good enough, not acceptable, not this and not that, then she's going to be in a position where she can use this meditation program to guide her to her own heart. And as she does this, she'll find that she can easily open her heart and accept the rest of the world just as it is.

We all tend to judge ourselves negatively, and this chronic, almost subliminal judgment definitely drags us down. Where does this habitual judgment come from? Usually we develop our underlying negative attitudes and core beliefs about ourselves early in childhood from our parents. This is one of the most terrible human characteristics—this tendency to pass down negative attitudes generation after generation, almost as if it's in our genes. But it isn't. Our negative beliefs are in our core assumptions about what life is all about and who we are.

Meditation is the most effective tool for looking deeply within ourselves to see the negative programming that we picked up in our early lives. It is also the ideal tool for challenging these negative attitudes so that we can replace them with more realistic and positive attitudes that will enable us to sing in our hearts rather than weep.

We are at a very hopeful point in history. We're right on the cusp of a major revolution in our society. More and more people are realizing that they can dramatically change the quality of their lives for the better if only they learn how to pause to see the negative thoughts that habitually run through their minds, act to quiet them, and replace them with more positive ones.

The wonderful spiritual master Krishnamurti says it this way: "Unless there is a deep psychological revolution, mere reformation on the periphery will have little effect. The psychological revolution, which I think is the only revolution, is possible through meditation."

As we move beyond judgment, we discover the truth that every human being by nature is a beautiful creation. We certainly distort this beauty through beliefs and thoughts that make us feel ugly and worthless and hopeless and so forth, but underneath, deep down, we're all magnificent creatures, if only we learn to let our little light shine in the world.

What about when you experiment with moving into meditation and looking into your heart, what do you usually find? Are you hurting inside from self-judgments, are you feeling empty or in despair, hopeless and frustrated and angry and all the rest? If so, the cure for these symptoms (for they are symptoms caused by underlying negative assumptions) is to continue returning to an inward focus of your attention, and to continue bringing more and more healing love into your heart and soul and mind.

The same is true of your relationship with your parents. You might want to pause for a few moments now and see what happens when you bring, for instance, your mother to mind. First of all tune into your breathing, your heart, your whole body presence. Now bring your mother's presence to mind and see if you can open your heart and accept her just the way she is, or if there are old judgments and rejections that stand between you and your potential to love your her unconditionally. If you find judgments, just observe them, and when you're ready, see how you feel toward your mom when you let these judgments go and accept her just as she is.

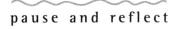

pause and reflect

CHAPTER 23
Walking the Path Together

Kent watched his mother as she went walking with a smile into the house, talking brightly with Danny's dad. He hadn't seen her so bright for months, and it made him feel very good inside. For so long she'd been totally busy just being a mom and holding down her job as leader of a tech-research team. She hadn't taken any time off for socializing in so long, and now, who knows, maybe there was a new romance in the making. Judging from how good it felt to be close with Lisa, Kent knew his mom would flourish again if she found a new man to love.

Dan was over scooping out chocolate ice cream from a half-gallon container, going for his second portion, which Kent thought was a great idea, so he went over with his bowl.

The girls were talking together way in the back of the big yard, while all the parents seemed to have disappeared into the house. Kent and Danny went with their ice creams over to the lawn chairs and sat there listening to the strange music that was now playing—a real cool acoustic guitar and some hand drums, and also what sounded like an Oriental flute of some kind, and some weird, high-pitched instrument.

"Peter likes his music strange," Danny said, "but I like most of it."

They sat and snarfed their ice cream down without talking for a couple minutes. "By the way," Kent said, "some people call you Dan and some Danny, which do you prefer?"

"Doesn't make any difference. I guess Dan sounds better these days. Hey, your mom seems to get along with my dad, that's a scary idea."

"She could use some social life," Kent said.

"Hmm."

"I wonder what they're talking about?" Kent said, nodding toward the two girls about a hundred feet away, sitting on the grass with their heads together.

"Oh, knowing them, meditation," Dan said.

"I never thought I'd end up doing something that weird. But hey, life's weird any way I look at it these days."

"You're telling me."

They sat a moment, not saying anything.

"But I like it," Kent said.

"What? Life?"

"Meditation. Lisa and I do it together."

"Yeah. Julie and me, too."

"This idea about meditation being something you do all the time, that's what's on my mind," Kent admitted. "I was working at the computer and suddenly I realized that I was like totally unaware of my breathing, of my body—just gone. So I tried to tune in, you know, with the focus phrases. It worked for a while, but I think the hardest thing to do, and still stay aware of your breathing, is work at the computer."

"So what, are you saying there's something inherently meditationally bad about computers?"

Kent laughed. "No, but you just try it. See how long you can stay aware of your breathing and work at the computer at the same time. Robert says we can do anything, and still be conscious of the here and now. Like, I was taking a test a couple of days ago and I was able to. And I think I did better than I would have otherwise—my mind was sharper."

"I still think it's kind of embarrassing," Dan admitted.

"Meditating?"

"Well, the whole thing of being some super-conscious Buddha right in the middle of playing Ping-Pong. But yeah, my game's getting better recently. Before I serve, I just inhale and tune in, and feel my feet on the floor and go whole-body, and I play better, no question. But what would people think if they knew what I was doing?"

"Well, like Lisa says, who cares, really?"

Dan eyed him. "You really like her, don't you," he said.

Kent grinned. "You bet. And you're not exactly upset at spending so much time with Julie."

"I can hardly believe how my life has changed in just a few weeks. My dad, too, he's getting better."

"What do you mean? He looks sharp to me."

"Oh, he had a down time, after my mom left."

"Hmm. I know that story."

"Scary—them seeming to like each other."

"It's been a little strange, me having a girlfriend, but Mom being alone. I hope your dad likes her."

"Ditto."

It was getting dark. Outside lights came on automatically here and there. The two girls got up and walked over to the two guys. Julie rested her hands on Dan's shoulders. Lisa did the same with Kent, and no one said anything. A night bird sang its solo tune off in one of the trees, almost as if playing along with the quiet jazz on the outside speakers.

"Hey, kids!" Lisa's mom shouted across the lawn to them from the back porch. "Want to come in? We'd like to talk with you about something."

"Uh, sure," Julie called back.

"Oh, so we're still kids," Kent said playfully. "Goats no doubt."

"My grandfather calls my father 'kid' sometimes," Julie said. "I guess they just never get over it."

"So what do you suppose the old folks are up to?" Dan wondered.

"With parents these days, you never can tell," Lisa put in. "I mean, sometimes it's hard to tell who the radical kids are around *here. Let's go see, shall we?"*

Inside they found the six parents sitting in the living room, the music just then switching to the jazz clarinet and Japanese flute of Music for Zen Meditation, *which made Julie and Dan smile to each other. The room was big and the four teenagers found places to sit.*

"Uh," said Peter.

"Well, uh what?" Julie prodded.

"Well, we were just talking about something, and we don't want to step on your toes or violate your space or anything," Peter went on uncertainly.

"Oh boy," from Dan. "You want to join the Ping-Pong team."

Everybody laughed.

"Actually," Julie's mom spoke up, "we've been asking Robert and Ruth if they might teach us something about meditation. We're all interested. I mean, we've seen how the four of you seem to like it. But we don't want to be pushing into your group or anything, so we're talking about having our own class once a week, it sounds like Wednesday evenings will be good. But we wanted to know what you think. I mean, it's your thing."

"Oh, right, we have the copyright on meditation," Julie joked. "But we can license it out to you, no problem."

"Dad," Dan said uncertainly, "you're interested?"

"Hey, I used to meditate a little in the old days," he said. "Until I met your mom and she told me meditation was of the devil. Sure, why not try it." He was sitting next to Veronica, and turned his head to look to her.

"So what do you think, Kent?" she asked her boy. "What we were talking about is a class for us oldies on Wednesday evenings, so that we can maybe catch up with you advanced meditators at some point. And also, maybe if you want, on Sunday mornings we can all get together, if that sounds good to all of you—just an idea."

The "kids" looked at each other, a bit puzzled by the sudden plans, but obviously pleased. They shrugged their shoulders and said, "Why not?"

"But wait," Kent said, looking to Robert. "I'll go along with this plot to infiltrate our inner circle only on one condition."

"Oh?" said Robert uncertainly.

"My condition is this: that right now, you tell us what the seventh focus phrase is. You only got to number six at our last meeting."

Robert laughed. "Oh, that's a tough condition, but why not. Here's your final piece of the puzzle, and it's actually designed to bring you right around in a circle, or a spiral, to where you started. So if you want, you can go another round, deeper and deeper, or higher and higher, up and down are about the same thing in meditation. It's actually more a matter of expansion from the center, than direction."

"Well, you definitely sound like you can teach this stuff," Veronica said.

"I know parts of the story," Robert admitted. "But what's most important, of course, is what you find for yourself."

"Hold on," Dan's father said, "I don't even know what a focus phrase is."

Robert nodded to Dan. "You tell him," he said.

Dan at first reacted to having the spotlight on him. But then he took a breath, looked to Julie, and just said what came to mind from his own experience. "There are seven steps to the meditation that Robert and Lisa and Ruth are teaching us," he said. "I don't think I could remember to do the whole flow of it, without the focus phrases. All you have to do is memorize the seven statements, and say them one after the other, and they point your mind's attention right where it needs to go to spark the next expansion."

"Hmm," from Dan's father. "I thought meditation was simple, just sitting there and doing nothing."

"When I just sit there and do nothing, I'm flooded with thoughts

nonstop," Dan said. "The focus phrases help the mind to look in directions that wake up all sorts of deep stuff. You'll find out when Robert and Ruth take you through it all. It's totally simple really; it just takes a couple of weeks of practice. And it helps when you have somebody talking you through it at first, to learn it by heart."

"Okay," Kent said, "we have a tournament downstairs scheduled for tonight, don't we? I want to see Dan wipe out Peter! Now how about that final focus phrase?"

Robert nodded. "Okay, and here's a taste of what's to come for the old folks. First, as in most meditations, you turn your attention toward your own immediate breath experience by saying 'I feel the air, flowing in and out, through my nose.' After tuning into that for a breath or two, or a dozen, doesn't matter, you expand your awareness to focus on two sensory experiences at once, by saying to yourself 'I feel the movements in my chest and belly as I breathe.' And after experiencing this expansion a while, you say 'I'm aware of my heart right in the middle of my breathing,' and let whatever emotional pressure you have inside you come flowing out with each exhale. At this point, with your mind focused on several inside happenings at once, thoughts have mostly calmed down in your mind, and you say 'My mind is now quiet.'

"So that's the first half of the meditation, just bringing you into a quiet, calm, expansive consciousness. A lot of meditations stop here, but we go further. The next step is to openly encourage acceptance and love, beginning with our own selves, by tuning even deeper into the heart and saying 'I love myself just as I am.' Remember, these phrases point toward where you want to move to, they're not just blind affirmations. They encourage expansion in the direction of the suggestion.

"The sixth step is important because it expands us beyond our personal bubble of awareness and opens our hearts to receive love and wisdom and healing from the infinite spiritual realms of the universe, by whatever name you choose to call God. The statement is:

'My heart is open to receive God's healing help.' And in the act of saying this, you'll feel your heart in fact opening and receiving.

"Okay, now what's the seventh, where do you go once you're totally expanded and in harmony and union with the infinite divine? The seventh statement moves you to where you can either just stay in this deep meditative state for however long you want or if you feel your thinking mind starting to get active and pull you off into thoughts about the past or the future, you can continue in the spiral and return to the first focus phrase where, in your already pretty deep state of meditation, you can again point your attention to that primal experience of breathing by saying 'I feel the air flowing in and out through my nose.' You can then continue through the seven expansions another time. It's a remarkably effortless process once you learn it by heart."

"But wait, the seventh focus phrase!" Kent insisted.

"Oops," said Robert, maybe playing with him a bit by still not having said it. "Actually, the seventh focus phrase just acknowledges the deep state the first six expansions have moved you into. Once you've opened your heart and soul to divine inspiration and healing and all the rest, you naturally move into peace and bliss. And so you say 'I am here . . . now . . . in bliss.' And like I said, you either stay there in meditation for as long as you want, or you return to the beginning and move through the spiral expansion again. And that's it!"

Peter jumped to his feet. "Okay, now for that tournament downstairs!"

And so we come full circle, with all seven focus phrases in hand. Sometimes you'll find that your mind prefers to move through the seven phrases fairly quickly, even once for each breath. Sometimes you'll find that you take five minutes to tune into each of the expansions. Sometimes you'll tune into your breathing and just stay with that experience for the whole meditation, as Buddhists do in Vipassana meditation.

This open-form approach to meditation is always a jazz performance on your part, because you're free to let your current mood and time frame move you through the seven expansions in a new way each time you pause to meditate.

What's vital is that you memorize and truly learn by heart the seven expansions, so that you have this basic structure and natural flow to guide you. Otherwise, all too often, thoughts intrude and take over the meditation. The focus phrases are your seven trusty beacons of light, guiding you to harbor. Once you move through the process a number of times you'll find that you internalize the seven statements and have them as your lifelong path to infinite exploration.

In our story it's certainly heartwarming to see both generations interested in learning how to focus inward and tune into their shared source of love, wisdom, and unity. As psychologists separate the mental process of meditation from its various religious traditions, we're free to advance into an era of human exploration in which we all have the mental tools to transcend inherited attitudes and embrace a deeper quality of consciousness that can bring our hearts and souls together into one community.

In this spirit, we see Julie, Lisa, Dan, and Kent learning firsthand what it means to go deep, to feel more deeply, and to love to their depths. We also have seen how their nonpushy living example of what meditation can bring into one's life spreads naturally to those around them. Sure, they will have to move regularly through obstacles on their journey to their depths. That's life. But they now have the tools to help them through their obstacles. Especially with the guidance of the seven short but powerful focus phrases; no matter where they are or what they're doing, they can keep returning to their inner core of being, and keep bringing more and more love and acceptance and bliss into the world.

And here you are, learning the same focus phrases, and experimenting with your own capacity to look inward, discover who you really are—and let your light shine more brightly in the world. You're bound to encounter your own doubts and confusions when you have difficulty focusing inward. You're bound to have times when you look inside and it hurts emotionally. Furthermore, you live in the most distracting life imaginable, with television and radio and all the media hype constantly trying to grab your attention and keep you away from your meditative potential.

But in the very midst of this most frenetic media culture of all time, here you are right now, consciously gathering the mental tools you'll need to help you just say no to all that distracting media hype. Most important, you're discovering that you and you alone are the master of your mind, and that you possess the power to regularly focus on inner realms that nurture your soul.

But we mustn't judge such things as the media, no matter how heartless it might appear. Along with all the soulless bombardments that have come with the electronic and computer revolution, we are also blessed with positive extensions of our nervous system, through the Internet and various outlets that are just now learning to employ media in ways that nurture.

Who knows where this will all lead. But as long as we keep our minds open to deeper guidance, our hearts full of love, and our souls receptive to wisdom, we should find that all the potential scientific expansions of consciousness can be used to spread compassion and wisdom and interconnectedness among the world community.

> For right now, what might you be feeling? How is your heart doing today? What attitudes and worries might be pulling you down and out of the present moment? And what happens when you employ the focus phrases to bring yourself fully "here" into the present moment?

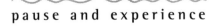

pause and experience

MEDITATION FOUR
Insight and Discovery

Let's become quiet, settle down, and step by step move through the seven focus phrases as we open to the full experience of unique expansion, with each new step, saying . . .

"I feel the air, flowing in and out, through my nose."

"I feel the movements in my chest and belly as I breathe."

"I'm aware of my heart right in the middle of my breathing."

"My mind is now quiet."

"I love myself just as I am."

"My heart is open to receive God's healing help."

"I am here . . . now . . . in bliss."

And as you experience deep peace and whatever new insights might come to you, continue to breathe, allow peace to fill your heart, and be open to receive.

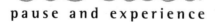

pause and experience

Part Five
SPECIAL COOL-CALM MEDITATIONS

In this section I review the meditations you've learned so far and teach you five new special "Cool-Calm" meditations. Whenever you want to focus on a particular theme discussed in this book, you can employ one of these special focuses during your next meditation. Meditation is a very powerful tool for resolving life issues, so feel free to regularly pause and consider if it might be worthwhile to move through one of these five special meditations during your next meditation.

Quick Meditation Uplift
(1 minute)

Let's become quiet, settle down, and step by step move through the seven focus phrases as we open to the full experience of unique expansion, with each new step, saying:

"I feel the air, flowing in and out, through my nose."

Breathe . . .

"I feel the movements in my chest and belly as I breathe."

Breathe . . .

"I'm aware of my heart right in the middle of my breathing."

Breathe . . .

"My mind is now quiet."

Breathe . . .

"I love myself just as I am."

Breathe . . .

"My heart is open to receive God's healing help."

Breathe . . .

"I am here . . . now . . . in bliss."

And as you continue to breathe, allow peace to fill your heart, love to heal your soul, and be open to a new experience.

The Basic Cool-Calm Meditation
(10 minutes)

Make sure you're comfortable. Stretch and yawn all you want. Now, gently turn your mind's focus to your breathing. Make no effort to breathe, just "be" with your breathing experience for a few breaths, feel the air rushing in and out your nose or mouth with each new breath.

Expand your awareness to also include the movements in your chest and belly as you breathe. Be aware of your whole body, here in this present moment.

Allow your awareness to expand to include your heart. Relax your tongue, your jaw, let your emotions flow out if they want to, accept yourself just as you are right now.

And say to yourself: 'I love myself just as I am."

Your thoughts now quiet, your breathing relaxed and free.

You can go ahead now and expand your personal awareness to include your deeper source of sustenance and love by saying to yourself: "My heart is open to receive God's healing help."

Stay with your breathing, your heart open to receive insight and wisdom, be open to a new experience.

When you're ready you can begin to move a little. Yawn if you want to, bring whatever insight and love has come with you as you open your eyes, stay aware of your breathing, of your whole body here in this present moment.

As you go about your day, allow the inflow of wisdom and love to continue, remain honest in your heart, clear and nonjudgmental in your mind, and open to allow your light to shine and touch everyone you meet.

Intuition: Resolving Life's Problems

There's no way to completely avoid difficulties, confusions, conflicts, and emotional upsets as we move through life. And the high school years seem especially wrought with a nonstop barrage of them. With each problem come decisions and choices we must make, and how we approach making these choices determines a great deal about how our lives will unfold.

If we make a decision while our minds and hearts are gripped with anxiety and confusion, we can make the wrong decision. But if we can learn how to drop down into a deeper place of acceptance and wisdom in our minds and hearts, we can make our decisions from a spiritually grounded perspective.

This meditation enables you to bring to your daily meditation whatever problem you might be struggling with, and help you to make the decisions you need to make in life from the very depths of your being. In this meditation you can tap into your full intuitive power to see your situation as a whole, and then respond to the situation from your heart, employing your whole mind as well as the wisdom of greater spiritual consciousness.

The flow of this Intuition meditation is easy to learn because you start out just as you do in the basic meditation, tuning into your breathing and heart using the focus phrases, until you reach the point where your heart is open to receive. At this point you simply expand the meditation so that it sheds special light and insight upon your particular problem.

You can spend as much time as you want focusing on your question, there's no time frame here. What's important is that you reflect upon your dilemma in an expanded meditative way, without anxiety about the future, without any pushiness from your thinking mind; instead, you open up to higher insight and remain in receive mode rather than think-think mode. This meditation is designed for insights to regularly come popping into your mind, and of course, that requires that you be open to receive rather than caught up in your own thoughts.

This is not to say that the thinking and plotting function of your mind isn't valuable. I'm sure that before you bring a problem to meditation for insight and resolution, you will have already have tried to find a solution—and were unsuccessful. You've considered all the usual solutions, you've played out imaginary scenarios of how the future might unfold to resolve your dilemma, but you're still confused, uncertain, torn by two or more different directions and choices you could make.

This is where meditation fits in beautifully. As you quiet all your busy and usually anxious/tense thoughts and expand your consciousness with the basic meditation that you have already learned, you tap into the higher intuitive and spiritual dimensions of consciousness. You are now open to receive flashes of insight and are attuned to that feeling in your heart where it knows the right decision has come to you. Now you can go into action and walk the heart path to a good-feeling resolution of your dilemma.

Let me guide you through this meditation now so that you get a feel for the power it brings when you need insight into the uncertainties and problems in your life.

To begin the meditation, go ahead and move a bit, stretch if you want to, and get entirely comfortable. Give yourself permission to temporarily let go of all your problems. Just ease up and relax into this present moment.

Notice your breaths naturally coming and going; tune into the sensation of the air flowing in and out through your nose or mouth with every new breath. Now expand your awareness to also experience the rhythmic movements in your chest and belly as you breathe.

Make no effort to inhale or exhale. Let your breathing stop when it wants to and start when it wants to, and after your breathing stops, notice the spark of life deep within you that again brings the air rushing in and out, through your nose or mouth. Go ahead and set your breathing free.

Now, as you stay aware of the breathing sensations in your nose and chest and belly, expand your awareness another step, this time to include the feelings in your heart, right in the middle of your breathing.

Begin to notice if your heart feels good or if there's any tension, pain, or pressure inside your chest. Accept what you find. Be your own best friend and be loving toward yourself. Say to yourself: "I love myself just as I am."

Now tune into the feelings in your throat. Let your tongue relax, and your jaw muscles. Breathe through your mouth if you feel under pressure inside. Make any sounds that express what you feel, and with each new exhale, let the pressure and feelings come rushing out and be released. Whatever feelings you find inside you, set them free—love them and let them go.

When you're ready, calm yourself down inside. As your breathing lets go of emotions and settles into a more relaxed rhythm, allow your breathing to flow more smoothly with each new inhale and exhale. Your mind is now quiet. You're at peace.

In the middle of this calmness, while you hold the primary focus on your breathing and whole-body awareness, begin to include in your focus of attention the question you want to reflect upon and seek guidance in resolving. You don't need to start thinking about the specific dilemma you want to resolve. Your mind knows full well the situation. All you need to do is stay with the feelings in your heart, stay aware of your breathing, and at the same time open yourself to allow new ideas and insights to come flowing into your mind.

Stay with your breathing as central, and say to your heart: "My heart is open to receive wisdom and guidance to help me with my situation."

Stay with this focus in your expanded awareness and allow insights to pop into your mind at their own speed—there's no hurry, just breathe and let the insights flow into your mind.

Now, when you're ready, try to clarify any insights or decisions or choices that have come to you, express them in a sentence or two so you'll remember your insights fully after the meditation.

Now you can just relax into the experience of being alive here in this present moment—nothing to do right now, nowhere to go, just the air flowing in and the air flowing out, your mind alert, your heart full of love, your soul at peace. Let the good feelings flow through you.

When you are ready open your eyes, stretch a bit, and end the meditation. Carry with you into the world your new insights about what to do in your life.

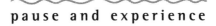

pause and experience

Emotions: Calming Anger and Worries

Regardless of who we are, no one is immune from recurrent bouts of upset emotions. Often when we sit down to meditate we find that our emotions are too explosive or anxious or depressed to allow us to move into deep meditative calm and peace. What can we do when we find ourselves unable to enjoy the present moment?

We've already seen the general meditative solution to feeling emotional pressure during meditation. As we tune into our breathing we immediately come into contact with our emotional pressures because they are expressed continually and directly in our breathing. Likewise, when we tune into our hearts, we encounter the emotions that are dominant in our lives at that time as well as the more buried ones that continue to grab at us.

Simply by focusing our mind's attention toward our feelings, we encourage release and healing of those emotions. The basic meditation regularly takes us through this process. But what should we do when one emotion dominates? Here is a special meditation that you can turn to whenever emotions are driving you crazy and you need devoted loving attention:

> As before and always, begin by moving a bit. Stretch if you want to, get entirely comfortable, accept how you feel even if something is upsetting you. Just be there with your emotions without fighting them, and as best you can, tune into and relax into this present moment.
>
> Even if your breathing is tense or agitated, tune into the sensation of the air flowing in and out through your nose or mouth with every new breath. Expand your awareness to include the movements in your chest and belly as you breathe.

See if you can set your breathing to stop when it wants to and start when it wants to.

As you stay aware of your breathing, expand your awareness to include the feelings in your heart, right in the middle of your breathing. Accept what you find—this is you right now.

Go ahead and breathe through your mouth if you're under emotional pressure; relax your tongue and jaw and begin to let your emotions flow out.

If you're angry, say so: "I'm angry!"

If you're depressed, say so: "I'm totally unhappy."

If you're anxious or worried, say so: "I'm feeling afraid."

If there is anger inside you, make any sounds you want to in order to let that anger express itself.

If there's sorrow inside you, let the tears flow if they want to.

If you're afraid or worried, experience the contractions in your breathing and heart.

Just fully be with your feelings without blocking or judging them. Let it all come flowing out. And stay tuned into your breathing throughout—it is your healing lifeline.

Now, complete the following sentence to express why you're feeling like you are: "I'm feeling so upset, because . . ."

Sometimes a particular person is the cause of your upset feelings. If there is someone you blame for your upset feelings, bring this person to mind. Imagine this person standing right in front of you. Give yourself permission to start talking to this person and tell her how you feel—really express your feelings to this person!

Now, to play fair, allow this person to give her side of the situation. Imagine this person talking to you, explaining how she sees the conflict or situation. Let her talk till she has expressed all of her feelings.

Now respond to what she has said, and as you do so, allow your feelings to perhaps change, to begin to heal and evolve into new feelings for this person.

Okay, you can let go of imaginations, just tune fully into your breathing and your heart at the same time. If your eyes are closed, perhaps open them a moment now, and look around the room.

Notice that, right now, there's probably nothing at all disturbing you. You're safe, no one is doing anything bothersome to you, nothing terrible is happening. In fact, everything in this present moment is okay in your life. As you breathe, tune into this present moment, recognize that you're okay and that you can choose to let go of the emotions, at least for now, and enjoy this moment.

And as your breathing begins to ease up and expand, you're free to continue with the meditation and open yourself up to some deep emotional healing as you say to yourself, "I love myself just as I am."

And with your mind quiet and your emotions calmer, you can say to yourself: "My heart is open to receive God's healing help." And with each new effortless breath open up to receive unconditional love. Let your thoughts and emotions receive healing as you let go of judging the world and blaming other people, and choose to feel good in your heart right now as love flows in and heals your pains and upset emotions.

Just relax into the experience of being alive here in this present moment. You have nothing to do right now, nowhere to go. The air is flowing in and the air is flowing out. Your mind is alert, your heart full of love, your soul at peace, and your emotions calm and satisfied.

When you're ready, open your eyes, stretch a bit, and end the meditation. As you go about your day, carry these brighter feelings with you to light up all that you do.

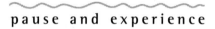

pause and experience

Relating: Healing Heartbreaks

Almost no one gets through high school without having their heart broken at least once. There's nothing more crushing than falling intensely in love with someone, experiencing that universal mystic union with another heart, and then getting rejected and discarded. No matter what the reasons or circumstances, broken hearts leave us shattered on all fronts.

Psychologically, the agonizing intensity of a romantic heartbreak has its source way back in early childhood and even in our genetic programming. We instinctively bond deeply in our hearts with our parents, to the extent that we actually feel one with them in our heart. Their center and our center seem the same.

We also instinctively fear being abandoned by our mother, or our primary nurturing parent. Why? Obviously because way back in early times a baby abandoned by its mother in the wilds almost always perished. So the fear of abandonment runs to the core of our being and is ultimately the fear of death.

This is why when we fall in love as young adults, and bond with a new person deeply in our hearts to where our emotional personal centers seem to merge, we tend to also activate our primordial fears of being abandoned by this person. In the nonlogical levels of our minds, we come to equate romantic rejection with our instinctive fear of being abandoned and, ultimately, dying.

This understanding of our fear of abandonment offers at least one solid explanation as to why we feel and behave so irrationally when we're in love, and especially when we are rejected and our heart gets broken. Jealousy also springs from this instinctive fear of losing our primary heart bond. We come to fear that we can't continue to exist if we lose our loved one. What makes matters worse, these fears are irrational, and therefore we can't readily use our logical minds to break free from the agony of heartbreak.

Once the basic psychological dynamic of the devastating experience of heartbreak is understood, we can approach the heart-healing process in a way that enables us to quickly recover. There is certainly no instant cure for heartbreak. It takes time to regain our center. But in meditation we can accelerate the recovery process and reduce the inner pain considerably.

At the core of spiritual awakening we always come to the beautiful realization that we are indeed being sustained and nurtured by a love that transcends earthly dimensions. The love of God by whatever name provides us with our eternal life-link with the infinite divine. I say these words not for you to disagree or agree, by the way, but for you to look within and discover for yourself.

Our hearts heal during meditation, from my understanding, because we accept honestly what has happened to us; we remember to love ourselves so that we can regain the inner center that we have given to another human being. And we open our hearts to receive love that will never leave us. It's no wonder that so many religions had a female mother figure at the heart of their teachings and prayers, for such deities represent the infinite care and protection and love that comes flooding into our hearts when we open up and receive.

And that's what we're going to do in this special "healing heartbreaks" meditation. Whenever you're feeling knocked flat romantically, whenever you feel depressed and unloved, whenever you find your heart aching or your inner center lost in another person's heart, you can turn to this meditation and begin the healing process.

Once again and as always in the beginning of a meditation session, make sure you're comfortable. Stretch and yawn all you want, accept how you feel, and gently turn your mind's focus to your breathing. Make no effort, just "be" with your breathing experience for a few breaths, with zero motivation.

Feel the air rushing in and out your nose or mouth. Expand your awareness to include the movements in your chest and belly as you breathe. Feel gravity pulling down on your body, holding you in the earth's gentle embrace. Listen to the sounds around you, be aware of your whole body, here in this present moment.

Now allow your awareness to expand to include, right in the middle of your breathing, your heart and all its feelings—no effort to breathe. Breathe through your mouth if you feel emotional pressure; relax your tongue, your jaw, and let your emotions flow out if they want to. Make sounds perhaps to express your feelings.

Now you can just relax. Continue to stay tuned into your breathing, your heart, your whole body's presence right here and now. If you want to, express how you feel in your heart. Say out loud, at whatever volume you want, whatever words express how you feel right now.

In this meditation, focused as it is on healing heartbreaks, we look deeper into how you feel and what happened to you that broke your heart. First of all, who broke your heart? Say his or her name, say "_____ broke my heart!"

Now notice how you feel about this person. Are you angry, depressed, accepting? Look and really see the hurt feeling inside you. Where is it? What is it? Stay aware of your breathing and look to see the truth of your broken heart.

Now let's look to see what assumptions, thoughts and beliefs are perhaps continuing to agitate your emotional wound. There are always one-liners running through our minds that continue to provoke heartbroken feelings. Perhaps you're thinking "I can't live without him," or "Nobody loves me, I'm unlovable," or "I hate that person!" or even "I want my mom!" Just stay aware of the pain in your heart, and watch what thoughts come flowing through your mind related to that inner pain.

Now let's see if you're ready to let go of the past, allow healing to take place, and reclaim your own inner center and your ability to stand on your own. Just watch the air flowing in and out your nose or mouth, the movement in your chest and belly as you breathe, and your heart beating right in the middle of your breathing. Your mind is now quiet. You're aware of your own self—alone and self-sufficient—and you can begin to regain your own inner center by saying "I love myself just as I am" a few times, so that the words begin to reawaken that good feeling of being content inside your own skin.

Now you can expand another beautiful step by saying to yourself: "My heart is open to receive God's healing help".

As you stay aware of the feelings in your heart, notice how with each new inhale you bring in the healing help from the infinite loving source of all life. Let the love flow in and soothe you. Allow the pain of heartbreak to flow out with each new exhale. Let the peace of God's love fill your heart as you surrender to whatever life brings you. Open your heart again to love.

When you're ready, begin to tune into the room around. Open your eyes, stretch a bit, and notice how you feel in your heart.

As you end this meditation, continue to hold in your heart the deep love you've found and spread this love wherever you go today. Lovingly hold your own center within you, and share your love with everyone you meet—until a new love comes your way and romance again flourishes in your life.

pause and experience

Love: Opening to Deep Sharing

It seems in our culture that we expect everybody to be able to grow up and somehow magically know how to successfully create and sustain a deep love relationship, as if it's the easiest thing in the world to do. The truth is that deep friendships and sexual relationships are vastly complex and all too often explode in our faces and cause great emotional pain that can not only continue for years but affect future relationships.

In the Relating Meditation we explored how to best heal an old relationship wound. In this meditation we are going to consider what you can do, in meditation, to prepare yourself for a new successful relationship and also how you can nurture that relationship after you've found a new true love.

We've talked about how dangerous it can be to leap into a deep relationship and totally merge your heart and soul with that new person. All too often, when we get too close and lose our own separate identity, we suffocate in the relationship and regress back to almost-infantile behavior and emotions. Then the ugly side of love appears in the form of possessiveness, jealousy, hostility, anxiety, and dependency.

The truth is, we can't ever have the same closeness, as adults, with a lover or friend as we had with our mother as an infant. Sure, we want it—that ultimate feeling of being one with another person who totally loves and cares for and protects us. But reality must be faced, and the desire for total oneness with another person must be let go of if we're to have healthy adult relationships.

The meditation you're about to learn is designed to help you look at yourself and your special loved one in the light of reality. Especially, this meditation will encourage you to regularly reestablish your own separate center in your own heart, to feel complete and whole and happy alone. Then and only then can you really love another person without being possessive and fearful of losing your love object.

There's a technical term for the fear of losing the love of someone you are close to: attachment anxiety. This is what you want to avoid in your new relationships of whatever kind. Even if you love your new car and feel attached to it, you're going to generate attachment anxiety because you fear losing it.

As soon as you identify with something beyond your own soul and physical body you are setting yourself up for the emotional pain of attachment anxiety. And here's the point of this meditation: Why put yourself in the position of having to suffer through all the inner agonies involved in the inherent uncertainty of forever holding on to something that you can't live without?

Meditation teaches us by inner experience two vitally important things. First of all, we are distinct separate bubbles of consciousness—each of us independent and responsible for our own feelings, thoughts, and spiritual development. Second, we have the ability to expand our personal bubble of awareness and interact with other people at deep heart levels, and ultimately merge with the infinite source of love and creation.

In this meditation we're going to consciously exercise our ability to move back and forth between total individual integrity, and a total merger of our hearts and souls with loved ones and God. A regular pulsation between these two extremes represents a healthy relationship—this is so important to learn! As long as you regularly retreat into your own independent presence and allow your loved one to come and go, to be free and not bound in your relationship, you can avoid the jealous anxieties that so often destroy an otherwise wonderful love relationship.

When you fall in love, naturally you bring some of your parents' programming about sexual love with you into your relating. This is natural but often not very helpful, because so many parents suffer from exactly what we're talking about. Many adults live their entire lives caught up in attachment anxiety related to their mates—what a shame!

But you don't have to carry on negative family traditions. In meditation especially you can observe the distorted one-liners that you inherited from your parents about what love is all about, see them run through your mind—and blast them with the light of reason and your own experience. You can also step by meditative step bring new attitudes and understandings about life to the fore of your consciousness, and leave behind attitudes that lead to fear and judgment, pain and conflict.

The bottom line is this: As soon as you become attached to something, anxiety is born, because almost nothing is permanent. Life is the constant process of letting go of the old and opening to receive the new. Even in a relationship with the same person over the years, that person continues to change. And you must allow that person to freely expand and grow and change if your relationship is going to endure.

Let's take a look at the actual meditation that will truly prove a lifeline in your relationships if you take it to heart and regularly practice it. Even when you're not in a deep love relationship, be sure to pause once a week or so to do this meditation, and make sure you're not clinging to anything out there for your sense of inner security.

Instead, as we learn so beautifully in meditation, regularly look inward to your own infinite core of being for your security. And open up to God's infinite love as your primary source of nurture and love. In this regular act, you'll charge yourself with love that you can then share with your loved ones—this is the model that meditation teaches us. Jesus said, "Love one another as I have loved you," and he surely loved in this nonattached way that gives everyone breathing space to grow without feeling confined by your needs and attachment.

Okay, enough talk; on to the main event! The first part of any meditation should by now ring in your ears as a mantra or beginning song that you always sing, that moves you effortlessly through the portal of the mind and into your deeper consciousness, where you can then direct your attention in specific helpful directions.

Once again and as always in the beginning, make sure you are comfortable. Stretch and yawn all you want. Let go of judgments and accept how you feel right now. Gently turn your mind's focus to your breathing. Make no effort to breathe, just "be" with your breathing for a few breaths.

Feel the air rushing in and out your nose or mouth. Expand your awareness to include the movements in your chest and belly as you breathe. Feel gravity pulling down on your body, holding you in the earth's gentle embrace. Listen to the sounds around you. Be aware of your whole body, here in this present moment.

Now, allow your awareness to expand to include, right in the middle of your breathing, your heart with all its feelings. Make no effort to breathe. Breathe through your mouth if you feel emotional pressure. Relax your tongue, your jaw, and let your emotions flow out if they want to. Make sounds to express your feelings.

Relax and continue to stay tuned into your breathing, your heart, your whole body presence right here and now. Say to yourself: "I love myself just as I am" as you open up to yourself as your own best friend.

Experience your inner capacity to truly accept who you are. Remember that you can't love someone else beyond the love you feel for yourself, so just let go of all your self-judgments about not being good enough, about how you look, or what you've done. Give yourself full permission to love yourself just as you are.

As you accept yourself as your own best friend, you can experience that wonderful feeling, inside your own heart, of being okay just as you are. There's nothing to do; everything's okay just as it is. This is God's perfect creation. Enjoy the beautiful feeling of being an integral part of that perfect creation and with each new breath, bring in more love.

With each new breath, with your thoughts now quiet, calmly notice that right now you are sustaining yourself, you are perfectly balanced. Your breaths are coming and going. You're alert, here in this present moment, and you can take care of yourself. So ease up and relax, enjoy your independent power and clarity and dwell deeply within your own center. Be content, safe, and at peace with the world.

In this peaceful state of centeredness within your own inner infinite being, you can effortlessly expand your personal bubble to include your deeper source of sustenance and love, power and wisdom, by saying to yourself: "My heart is open to receive God's healing help."

Without any thoughts or expectations, just go ahead and let your heart open, and receive.

Now, within this infinite love and acceptance and wisdom, bring to mind someone you are, or want to be, close friends with. Stay with your breathing and your inner sense of completeness and wholeness and bring this person into your awareness and your spiritual bubble.

Let your love for this person expand with total acceptance, and zero dependence. Each of you is free and strong and loving. Say to this person: "I love you, without clinging to you. I love you."

When you're ready, begin to tune into the room around you. Open your eyes, stretch a bit, and notice how you feel in your heart.

As you end this meditation, continue to hold in your heart the deep love you have found, and spread this love wherever you go today as you lovingly hold your own center within you and share your love with everyone you meet.

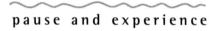

pause and experience

Wisdom: Discovering Who You Really Are

People often wonder what is the difference between someone who is smart and someone who is wise. We can be smart and also wise, and we can be smart and not very wise, and even wise without being so smart, but what does this really mean?

Intelligence (being smart) is a measure of cognitive capacity and is determined by how well we can process, memorize, analyze, and communicate data. Being smart also refers to how clever we can be in creatively reorganizing various data inputs and coming up with a unique solution to a problem.

Really smart people can do mental tricks that less-smart people simply can't. For instance, people with a high intelligence quotient (IQ) can often perceive seven different items at once and register all seven for future recall, whereas people with a lower IQ can only perceive, register, and remember maybe five different items at once. Really smart people can also perform many mental tasks rapidly and correctly, whereas people who are considered less intelligent don't perform so well.

In other words, being intelligent is a function of your cognitive machinery, your brain wiring, your genetic luck, and also your willingness to work hard with your cognitive system. Intelligence usually has no reference at all to anything having to do with the heart, with emotional strength or capacity, with spontaneous whole body response capability, or anything else unrelated directly to linear cognitive ability and prowess. Intelligence is a function of individual materialist ego performance.

Wisdom, on the other hand, emerges from an entirely different function of the mind. Wisdom is an outgrowth of years of inner reflection and observation such as happens in meditation. A person becomes wise rather than being born wise. Wisdom emerges not from the intellect of the brain but from the deeper experiential capacity of the intuitive function of the brain, and also the interaction of the brain with the heart.

It's hard to talk about the existence of wisdom that is not grounded in the heart, in deep honest feelings, in ever-expanding spiritual awareness, and in the centrality of love in one's life. Wisdom comes to us, we don't make it happen, nor can we manipulate it, as we can intelligence. Becoming wise is a process wherein we regularly put aside our prejudices and assumptions about what life is all about and simply look to see the truth of the matter even if it violates every law we've been taught.

Wisdom comes to us through our willingness to simply look, and see, what is true. And this experience of seeing and knowing the truth is a happening that surely includes the brain but always includes the heart as well. In all traditions, wisdom is spoken of as emerging from the heart, not the head. Many Native Americans spoke of the White Man as being entirely insane because the White Man thought with his head rather than his heart. In native traditions throughout the world, leaders were chosen not for their intelligence, which could often lead to terrible decisions, but for their wisdom, which could see to the heart of a situation and intuitively know what was the right action.

In our culture, we've almost lost the entire notion of wisdom when it comes to choosing leaders. Indeed, our political leaders often exhibit decision-making behavior that indicates almost no reflective long-term wisdom at all. We're in a dangerous situation right now, with so many political and business leaders—who are really sharp in their heads but seemingly so numb or asleep in their hearts—making such unwise decisions.

Wisdom almost always seems to include a sense of the long term, a feeling for what is right not just for the immediate moment but for future generations. Wisdom seems almost timeless in its sense of the overall flow of life. Wisdom involves a sense of depth and perspective that transcends the individual and the moment and includes the whole and the eternal.

This of course leads us to the question of spirituality and wisdom. I don't think wisdom can be separated from spirituality because they mean basically the same thing: the inclusion of a greater vision of what life is all about, and the capacity to transcend individual ego attitudes and perspectives so as to include a greater vista and vision. To be walking the spiritual path means to be steadily looking to see what is really real, and thus expanding one's capacity for wisdom.

It is often assumed that wisdom is a quality of the elderly, and indeed, if they've walked a life of awareness and love, many elderly people advance into a quality of wisdom that is very important and valuable for a culture, even if the culture fails to value that wisdom. I strongly encourage you to take the time to hang out with old folk who seem wise, and allow them to share with you their timeless insights into life.

Here's another curiosity: people think that wisdom just sometimes rather randomly appears in people. Wisdom in our culture is not something that we aspire to, nor is it something we consciously nurture within us.

Let's begin right here to reverse this false assumption. I personally don't think wisdom is a quality only of the elderly. I've known remarkably wise children. So have you, probably. These are children who aren't relating to the world out of fear or through their upbringing and cultural assumptions. These are children who are very conscious in the present moment, who respond with their hearts, and who are impeccably honest.

So often this wisdom of the very young is lost by the time a child reaches ten or twelve; it's been banged out of us by a society that demands conformity of thought, belief, and behavior. I'd like to initiate a great yet quiet and peaceful revolution by recommending that teenagers throw off the adult assumption that kids aren't capable of being wise in their thoughts and actions. I'd like to recommend also that you begin to consciously nurture your own wisdom by employing your daily meditation sessions to increasing your WQ—your wisdom quotient.

It's not at all hard to become more wise, whatever your age. All you need is what we've been learning throughout this book: to become conscious in the present moment; to tune into your heart as much as you can; to be as honest as you can, especially with yourself; and to become a constant observer of the world you inhabit every new moment of your life. And while you perceive the truth of what it means to be alive on this planet as a human being right now, also regularly open your heart to receive insight and love and healing and power from beyond your personal ego center. Keep your heart open to the inflow of the deeper truth of the universe, and let this deeper quality of consciousness freely flow outward so that you become a bright beacon of wisdom to those around you.

As you can already guess, being wise is not an act of the ego. You know a wise person immediately because they are humble rather than proud. They're in awe of the spiritual truths they know, and they know that their source of wisdom comes from beyond them.

In this spirit Lao Tzu, that truly wise ancient teacher from Taoist China, gave the following advice: "Yield and overcome; bend and be straight; empty and be full; have little and gain . . . therefore the wise embrace the One, and set an example for all. Not putting on a display, they shine forth. Not justifying themselves, they are distinguished. Not boasting, they gain recognition. Therefore be really whole, and all things will come to you."

Jesus likewise said, "The first shall be last, and the last shall be first." Also, he said, "Know the truth, and the truth will set you free." Buddha as well instructed his students to let go of their ideas about what life is all about, to simply observe without judgment, to see clearly—and that very act of seeing clearly, without anything else, will awaken wisdom in the heart.

The question now is how can we use meditation to be really whole and nurture wisdom within our own hearts, whatever age we might be? Let me guide you through the meditation, and you'll see for yourself.

Make sure you're comfortable; stretch and yawn all you want. Now gently turn your mind's focus to your breathing. Make no effort to breathe. Just "be" with your breathing experience for a few breaths.

Feel the air rushing in and out your nose or mouth. Expand your awareness to also include the movements in your chest and belly as you breathe. Be aware of your whole body, here in this present moment.

Now allow your awareness to expand to include your heart. Relax your tongue, your jaw, and let your emotions flow out if they want to. Say to yourself: "I love myself just as I am."

With each new breath, with your thoughts now quiet, calmly expand your personal bubble to include your deeper source of sustenance and love. Say to yourself: "My heart is open to receive insight and wisdom."

Stay with your breathing, your heart open to receive insight and wisdom.

Be open to a new experience.

When you're ready, begin to move a little, yawn if you want to, and without thinking, bring whatever has come to you with you as you open your eyes. Stay tuned into your breathing; your whole body here in this present moment.

As you go about your day, allow the inflow of wisdom and love to continue, as you remain honest in your heart, clear and nonjudgmental, open to allow your little light to shine and touch everyone you meet.

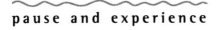

pause and experience

FINAL WORDS: MEDITATION IN ACTION

Throughout this book we've been exploring how meditation isn't just something we do once a day for half an hour; rather, meditation is a quality of consciousness that we nurture each and every moment so that we're optimally aware and heart-centered and spirit-guided in all that we do.

Of course, we do need regular daily practice to strengthen our ability to remain in a meditative state throughout the day. A daily solitary retreat is vital to developing the ability to stay in an expanded state of consciousness in all that we do. Hopefully you'll be able to find time each day to stop whatever you're doing and take a few minutes—or half an hour—to turn inward. Developing a regular habit of pausing and opening to your greater self is one of the most important goals you can aspire to.

The bottom line is this: Our society doesn't overtly support deep reflection and spiritual growth. And no one else is going to nurture your inner emotional well-being and spiritual growth. This is your responsibility. So the daily retreats are your time to optimize your training in meditation. This book is here to strongly support you in pausing at least once to look inward, tune into the present moment, open your heart to love and wisdom . . . and brighten your day.

As your inner light comes step by step to blaze more brightly and clearly with the infinite fire of compassion and wisdom, you'll find that everywhere you go, you can carry this spiritual flame into the world. Whenever you lose the flame and sink into negative emotions and thoughts, or if you suddenly realize that you have lost who you are, take the time to simply tune into your breathing and regain your inner light.

Exploring the Infinite

You might find, when you first begin to meditate, that you are spending days or even weeks not going very deeply into a meditative state. This is perfectly okay and often to be expected. In childhood we learn certain assumptions about what life is all about, and most of these assumptions are quite limiting. In meditation we learn how to open the doors of perception so that we see more clearly and more deeply into life, but this takes time.

The beautiful news is that you have your entire lifetime for spiritual exploration, so there's no hurry, and no need for impatience or pushing. You already have in hand all the basic meditational tools you'll need for your lifetime exploration. The techniques given here are not the only ones that you might find valuable, but I've done my best to put together a complete meditation program that will point you toward all the primary doors . . . and encourage you to open them.

But there's a twist to meditation and all things based on the heart rather than the mind: Pushing doesn't make the door open. All these inner doors will open in their own good time. You can ask the doors to open, and they will. But you can't use your will to make them open. This is the beauty of the spiritual path; it's effortless, and comes at its own pace.

Another giant dynamic of spiritual exploration is that God doesn't push either. Most of us go through life unaware of the greater spiritual dimensions of life because we have been given the freedom to shut our hearts to God (by whatever name); we live our lives entirely unconscious or in denial of the greater reality of this universe and beyond.

The infinite guidance of spiritual wisdom is always present and awaits those who ask for it. Meditation is the process of asking to receive, and that is why the sixth expansion, "My heart is open to receive," is so powerful. You are asking to receive. If you never ask, you will never receive. Jesus said, "Ask, and it shall be given to you; knock, and the door will open; seek, and you will find." Meditation is that process.

But here's the rub: Very often we ask, but with expectations of what we're going to find. These expectations limit us and often make our early meditations frustrating, because we're looking in the wrong direction.

We're awaiting the known, whereas in meditation we discover the unknown. So if you find that you're feeling frustrated with "nothing happening" in your meditations, it may be because you're entering into meditation expecting certain things to happen—celestial fireworks or a relief from a particular emotion.

Many people have deep wonderful experiences and feelings early in meditation, and then they try to make those experiences and feelings come back again and again. Be very careful of this pattern of wanting to repeat a spiritual performance, because it never happens!

By definition, every moment is new and unique; it's never happened before. So if you're looking for something that you've already experienced, you're going to sit there and find nothing. I can't overemphasize the importance of letting go of the known, as Krishnamurti encourages, so you can encounter and embrace the new. That's what meditation is all about.

So, as you explore the infinite, don't anticipate anything. Simply be open, calm, and experience the present moment. The Zen saying "Nowhere to go, nothing to do" perfectly expresses meditation. What we discover when we look honestly within is that we are already in paradise. We don't have to do anything to achieve spiritual awakening. Indeed, there is nothing we can do, because it comes as a pure gift, as a soft breeze blowing in through the window; spirit comes to us as a constant blessing when we are simply quiet, at peace, and centered lovingly within our own heart.

SHARING WHAT YOU LEARN

We are near the end of this book, and you've learned a lot about meditation, and hopefully spent time beginning to develop your inner capacity to pause at least once each day and take the time to nurture your inner potential. In the weeks and months to come, I hope you'll continue to deepen your meditative habit and look forward to each time you take a breather from your everyday routines to enter into meditation.

You have begun an inner journey that you can continue all your life as you explore the infinite realms of consciousness that meditation will open up to you. In this final section I share with you a few thoughts about how to support your own meditation practice, and also how best to share your growing interest and involvement in meditation with those around you.

Keeping a Meditation Journal

One of the best ways to support a daily meditation practice is to begin right away to keep a personal journal or diary related specifically to your experiences with meditation and your reflections upon those experiences. All you need is any kind of notebook that you'll enjoy writing in or a private file in your computer. Many people think it's better to keep a handwritten journal rather than to type one, but maybe that's just old-fashioned thinking. You decide for yourself where and how you want to write down your reflections.

One of the positive effects of keeping a journal is that when you begin each day's entry by writing down the day and the date, this helps you to develop a sense of each new day. Keeping a journal will also help you to schedule time each day to meditate. I can't overemphasize the importance of making the effort, especially in the beginning, to set aside a particular time in your daily schedule to just stop everything you're always so busy doing and take that essential breather to open up to nurture and receive.

There are various ways to approach a meditation journal. I'll give you some general ideas, and you can then do what you want each day. For instance, before they meditate, many people take five minutes or so to jot down whatever is on their minds and to note the main emotions inside them. By doing this before you meditate, you begin the process of tuning inward. You also get off your chest a lot of what perhaps is bothering you, so that your meditation can progress more easily and more deeply. Try writing in your journal a bit before you meditate and see if this is a step that feels good.

You can also write your honest feelings about meditation itself. Maybe you're having doubts that meditation is even worth setting time aside for. If you have these doubts, don't bury them; acknowledge them by writing them down. Maybe you remember something from the day before when you meditated, and you want to write down those reflections. Perhaps you have expectations about this day's meditation—write down whatever comes to mind!

You might also benefit from writing down each time, in the last twenty-four hours, that you paused, if only for a one-minute breather, and moved through the seven focus phrases, or perhaps just tuned into your breathing. Reflecting on how you are integrating meditation into your life will help you considerably in remembering to tune into your deeper self more and more often each day.

Just before putting your journal aside and meditating, you might want to write down what you especially want to do in meditation this day. Do you want to move through the seven focus phrases in the basic meditation, or is there a special theme you want to explore using one of the Special Cool-Calm Meditations? If so, make note of what you intend to do this day in meditation.

Then, of course, at a certain point you put the meditation journal away and enter into meditation. If you've learned the basic seven-phrase process by heart you simply close your eyes and off you go.

So you meditate, for five or ten or twenty or thirty minutes, depending on your schedule and desire. Then, as you gently emerge from your meditation session, don't immediately grab your meditation journal to make your entry. Take the time to hold your meditation experience close to your heart so that you don't lose the feelings you attained during your meditation.

When you do pick up your journal (if you want to after meditation as well as before), just sit for a few moments with it open and stay aware of your breathing, your heart, your whole body presence. See what words naturally come flowing out of you as you let your meditation experience emerge.

This phase of the meditation journal process can be immensely interesting and valuable, because after meditating and quieting the mind entirely, unexpected insights come flowing out of you from a very deep source. Listen to this wisdom as you write it down, and in this way you keep a record of the insights that come to you during and right after meditation.

The point here is that you are allowing your deeper voice to speak, and often, the process of writing enables this voice to speak most easily and clearly. Remember that this isn't a term paper you're writing; it's not something other people will read. You're expressing your own deeper feelings and insights. Writing is often a magical path through which our deeper selves can be heard.

Talking with Your Parents

We've seen in our story how, very often, parents somehow get involved when their children begin meditating. Your own family situation is unique, so you'll have to decide for yourself to what extent your parents might be open and interested in your new experiences with meditation.

What's important is to remember that no matter what our age, we're all in the process of learning about life. No one is ever too old to open up to something new, and your parents might surprise you when you share what you're learning through your new daily practice.

There is one thing to avoid, of course, and that's having the need for your parents to accept and even participate in your new venture. Meditation is not a religious cause that people go out and push to get new converts. The very nature of meditation is to grant all other human beings their own path, and not to get on the missionary bandwagon of trying to convert people to your belief.

The beauty of meditation is that it's not a belief at all, as we've seen. Meditation is all about experiencing reality, not about developing beliefs about reality. Certainly you can openly express your enthusiasm for what you're discovering in meditation, and your enthusiasm can ignite interest in those around you. I'm not in any way putting a damper on your eagerly talking about your new passion. All I'm suggesting is that you don't need converts in meditation. You alone in meditation represents a complete experience. If other people become interested, great—but remember that you are whole and totally at peace with the situation even if you're the only person in your whole school who meditates.

And as far as your parents go, they already have their beliefs in their heads; there's no point in trying to get them to change their minds—that's their business, not yours. Certainly don't keep it a secret that you're learning to meditate. Share with them whatever they're open to hearing. But don't be upset if they don't share your enthusiasm or if they think meditation is dumb or whatever. You will know in your heart from direct experience the truth of the matter.

As you continue to meditate and open up to greater realms of experience, who knows what will happen. This is the exciting thing about walking the spiritual path of the ever-emerging unique present moment: life becomes full of wonderful surprises!

Meditating with a Friend

One of the paradoxes of meditation is that it is an entirely solitary process usually done all alone in retreat and it is also a beautiful experience to share with someone. On the solitary side, you'll find that a daily meditation practice works best if you establish a quiet spot that you can return to each day, someplace where the outside world doesn't intrude upon your inner peace and exploration. On the sharing side, you'll perhaps discover kindred spirits at school or elsewhere who want to meditate with you. Both extremes are a blessing.

We've learned a lot from our story in this book about all the various dynamics of group meditation, be it with one other person or more than one person. Certainly one on one is a more intimate and remarkable addition to a friendship. Without being pushy, at some point you'll almost definitely feel the desire to meditate with one of your friends, or your parents, or your romantic partner. And when you do this, you'll find that your meditations are quite different from what they are when you meditate alone.

My advice is that if you participate in group meditations with friends, make sure you also maintain your daily solitary meditation practice. There's nothing quite like the solitary meditation experience, where you are entirely alone with your own inner presence.

When you meditate with a friend, you'll find that as you expand your consciousness, you naturally become aware of the other person, who is also expanding their consciousness to include you. This is the remarkable part of meditating with a friend—that your personal bubble of awareness expands to include the other person's presence, and a very deep sharing and sense of oneness is experienced. What a boost to true love, be it platonic or passionate, when you meditate together!

All too often, people start talking right after meditating. I would like to suggest that you do just the opposite; talk with your friend openly about this, so that it's clear. Make sure it's understood that you are going to stay quiet for at least a few minutes after meditating.

Certainly at some point sharing your experience is wonderful. Just make sure you emerge from meditation gracefully and quietly, so that you can continue to hold in your heart all the wisdom and love you received during meditation.

Also, be a little careful of not making meditation with your friend a "big thing." Sometimes your friend won't be as passionate about meditation as you are at the time, and this is fine; don't make a daily, shared meditation a requirement of a friendship, for instance. You have your personal commitment to your daily meditation retreat. Meditating with a friend is just an added blessing that might come and go less frequently than your daily solitary meditation. Take it as it comes, without holding on to any requirements with your friend.

Starting a Meditation Group

Meditation groups come into being almost spontaneously. You begin meditating by yourself, then a friend becomes interested, and then another friend wants to join your meditation—and voilà! You have a meditation group. What you'll find most important with such a group is that you help each other learn the basic meditation process, and perhaps all read the same book so you have the same reference point for the process. It's certainly fine to explore variations on the basic meditation theme. Just be sure that you have a common set of terms and understandings so you can talk with each other about your experiences.

Structure-wise, I have only very general suggestions, such as how helpful it is to establish a particular time and place, perhaps once or twice a week, for gathering together so that the logistics are easy to manage and a valuable group habit emerges. And when you get together, have a clear agreement as to how you like the flow of the meditation to move. For instance, at some point after you sit down together and chat a bit, you'll want to agree to no more talking for a set period of time. Twenty minutes is often a good time frame for meditation but it's also fine, in the beginning, to "sit" for just ten minutes—whatever you decide.

Sometimes a meditation group will have a leader at first, like Lisa, and then, as everyone masters the meditation, the need for a leader drops away. Just make sure that no one dominates the group, as so often tends to happen. Meditation, even in a group, needs to remain very much a free individual act.

Groups are curious creatures. People come and go, conflicts sometimes arise in terms of leadership and are resolved—you will learn a lot about group dynamics through being in a meditation group. What's important is remembering to relate from the heart, and not to try to manipulate anything. Meditation works in its own unique way.

Online Help and CD Programs

Hopefully, now that you've reached the end of this book, you're beginning to master the seven-step meditation by heart. Be sure to return to the beginning of the book and move again through each of the steps of the meditation, so that you truly make this meditation process your own—repetition is key for learning to meditate!

To help you in this learning process, I also invite you to also visit my multi-media website at www.johnselby.com where you'll find loads of help in learning to meditate. Especially, you'll be able to tap immediately (if you have broadband) into audio programs where you can listen to my voice guiding you through the CoolCalm meditations. Just click on the CoolCalm button on the left and you're in!

I also welcome you to listen to other meditations and programs on my website that will take you deeper and deeper into your own inner power and wisdom. The streamed-audio programs will enable you to just close your eyes, relax, and let me guide you through the learning process, until the meditations truly become your own. And you'll find other books that you can read online, plus meditation music and loads of other helpful stuff.

For when you want to be away from the computer and listen to the meditations on CD, there is a special CoolCalm Meditation CD I've recorded, that you can use anywhere. Just go online and order. You will find these CDs helpful both when meditating alone and also if you're meditating with a friend or starting a meditation group.

If you want to order by regular mail, you can send a check for $16 for the "CoolCalm Meditation CD" (cost covers handling and shipping) to:

CoolCalm CD
PO Box 861
Kilauea HI 96754

Also, if you have any particular questions you'd like me to help you with, or comments on your meditation experience, I do my very best to answer emails my readers send in—just go online to www.johnselby.com and click on the contact button. We're also working to set up chat rooms so you can talk with each other about your meditation experiences. I welcome you to a long-term friendship as we explore deep down and together, what it really means to be a human being on this planet and how we can enjoy life to the fullest, each and every new day. Enjoy your own awakening process (it's a lifetime exploration!) and spread the love and light and fun everywhere you go.

REFERENCES AND FURTHER READING

If you want to explore further reading on meditation, here are some of the very best books I know, divided into six sections based on specific interests. Most of the books that are listed with older publishing dates have new editions. Your library should have most of these books. Of course, there are also many other good books on these topics.

Yogic Hindu Meditation

Dass, Ram. *Journey of Awakening: A Meditator's Guidebook*. New York: Bantam Books, 1978.

Pinker, Steven. *How the Mind Works*. New York: W. W. Norton, 1997.

Rosenberg, Larry. *Breath by Breath: The Liberating Practice of Insight Meditation*. Boston: Shambhala Publications, 1998.

Teasdale, William. *The Mystic Heart*. Novato, Calif.: New World Library, 1999.

Yogananda, Paramahansa. *Autobiography of a Yogi*. Los Angeles: Self Realization Fellowship, 1987.

Buddhist Meditation

Austin, James. *Zen and the Brain*. Cambridge, Mass.: MIT Press, 1998.

Cleary, Thomas. *The Essential Tao*. New York: HarperCollins, 1991.

Das, Lama Surya. *Awakening the Buddha.* New York: Broadway/Bantam, 1997.

Goldstein, Joseph. *Insight Meditation.* Boston: Shambhala Publications, 1994.

Hanh, Thich Nhat. *Present Moment, Wonderful Moment.* Berkeley: Parallax Press, 1990.

Kabat-Zinn, Jon. *Wherever You Go, There You Are.* New York: Hyperion, 1994.

Kornfield, Jack. *A Path with Heart.* New York: Bantam, 1993.

Levine, Steven. *A Gradual Awakening.* New York: Doubleday, 1993.

Watts, Alan. *Still the Mind.* Novato, Calif.: New World Library, 2000.

Wei, Henry, trans. *Tao Te Ching.* Wheaton, Illinois: Theosophical Publications, 1988.

Christian Meditation

Harvey, Andrew. *Son of Man: The Mystical Path to Christ.* New York: Tarcher-Putnam, 1998.

James, William. *The Varieties of Religious Experience.* New York: University Books, 1963.

Katie, Byron and Stephen Mitchell. *Loving What Is*. New York: Random House, 2002.

Lewis, C.S. *Mere Christianity*. New York: Macmillan, 1943.

Merton, Thomas. *Contemplative Prayer*. New York: Doubleday, 1969.

Underhill, Evelyn. *The Mystics of the Church*. New York: Schocken, 1964.

Islamic Meditation

Andrae, Tor. *Mohammed: The Man and His Faith*. New York: Dover, 1955.

Buber, Martin. *Tales of the Hasidim*. New York: Schocken, 1947.

Cleary, Thomas. *The Essential Koran*. San Francisco: HarperCollins, 1993.

Helminski, Kabir. *The Knowing Heart: A Sufi Path of Transformation*. Boston: Shambhala Publications, 1999.

Nicholson, Reynold. *The Mystics of Islam*. London: Routledge Press, 1963.

Robinson, Neal. *Islam*. Washington D.C.: George Washington University Press, 1999.

Must-Read Classics

Bohm, David. *Wholeness and the Implicate Order.* Boston: Routledge, 1980.

Castaneda, Carlos. *Journey to Ixtlan.* New York: Ballantine, 1972.

Einstein, Albert. *Out of My Later Years.* New York: Philosophical Library, 1950.

Freud, Sigmund. *The Future of an Illusion.* New York: W. W. Norton, 1927.

Gurdjieff, G. I. *Meetings with Remarkable Men.* New York: Penguin, 1993.

Huxley, Aldous. *The Perennial Philosophy.* New York: Meridian, 1970.

Jung, Carl. *Memories, Dreams, Reflections.* New York: Fontana, 1995.

Krishnamurti, J. *The Awakening of Intelligence.* New York: Harper, 1973.

Krishnamurti, J. and David Bohm. *The Awakening of Intelligence.* New York: Routledge, 1999.

Russell, Bertrand. *Mysticism and Logic.* New York: Anchor Books, 1957.

Key New Books

Crowley, Vivianne. *Thorsons Principles of Jungian Spirituality*. New York: HarperCollins, 1998.

Newberg, Andrew, Eugene d'Agnili and Vince Rause. *Why God Won't Go Away*. New York: Ballantine, 2001.

Russell, Peter. *Waking Up in Time*. Novato, Calif.: Origin Press, 1998.

Selby, John. *Quiet Your Mind*. Hilo, Hawaii: Inner Oceans Press, 2004.

——. *Seven Masters, One Path*. San Francisco: HarperCollins, 2003.

Shapiro, Rami. *Wisdom of the Jewish Sages*. New York: Harmony Books, 1993.

Snyder, Gary. *Practice of the Wild*. New York: Farrar, Straus and Giroux, 1990.

Tolle, Eckhart. *The Power of Now*. Novato, Calif.: New World Library, 1999.